I LOVE MYSELF SO…

A Guide to Creating
A Life You Love

CORY JENKINS

DEDICATION

This book is dedicated to my mother who sent me to my first self-improvement, personal development and transformational education course.   I released this on her birthday, January 13th and it climbed the Amazon.com charts to number one in her honor.

She has supported and encouraged me through all of my crazy adventures and leaps of faith, including, but not limited to, writing my first book.

Happy Birthday Mom!
Love You Always

Our deepest fear is not that we are inadequate. Our deepest fear is that we are powerful beyond measure. It is our light, not our darkness that most frightens us. We ask ourselves, 'Who am I to be brilliant, gorgeous, talented, fabulous?' Actually, who are you not to be? You are a child of God. Your playing small does not serve the world. There is nothing enlightened about shrinking so that other people won't feel insecure around you. We are all meant to shine, as children do. We were born to make manifest the glory of God that is within us. It's not just in some of us; it's in everyone. And as we let our own light shine, we unconsciously give other people permission to do the same. As we are liberated from our own fear, our presence automatically liberates others.

~ Marianne Williamson

CONTENTS

Ask Yourself This...

What Would I Do
At This Moment
If I Truly Loved Myself?

INTRODUCTION

View from the top of Elephant Rock
Bountiful, Utah

As a young woman, I went through several of the trials that other young women went through, including the awkward stage of not really fitting in. I was constantly searching outside myself to fix what I thought was 'wrong' with me until I realized; *'I'm perfect just the way I am.'* Then and only then did the craving to fit in cease to be such a quest. However, that definitely took a long time.

People always ask me how I do the things that I do in my life.

I get questions such as:

How do you stay so positive?

Why is it that I never see you get angry?

How is it that you have friends all over the world?

How do you travel so much and to so many places?

What do you do for a living that gives you so much freedom?

How is it that you just keep going like the energizer bunny?

How can you sing and dance in front of people?

Why do I feel so comfortable around you?

Why do I feel like I can tell you anything?

I sometimes go to another person's event and people will start asking me where things are and what's happening because they think I'm the host. What is it about me that gives people that impression?

So many questions, so little time, but this book will answer many of them.

In my early twenties, my mom introduced me to Landmark Education and it was there I began my work in personal development. It was there that I met the woman who introduced me to Juice Plus and helped start me down the road to better health. This also got me interested in the study of nutrition. I was also introduced to a host of other educators such as Jim Rohn, Zig Ziglar, John Maxwell, Jack Canfield and several others who influenced my life in various ways.

My mother started this ball rolling in my life. I have her to thank for several discoveries and adventures in life and the feeling of freedom and the curiosity to experience and explore the world and meet new people. My Aunt Betty instilled in me the taste for the open road, a love of dance, and an example of someone doing what they want in their life. Her stories inspired me. My dad imparted to me his love of music, France, and the French language. Juice Plus, as well as other self-employment income, such as real estate investments, provided me with enough income to travel when I choose and the freedom to work from wherever.

Over the years, I developed the mindset that I would always find rewarding opportunities like these; opportunities that supported and enabled me to go for my dreams and reach my goals. Thanks to that mindset, I've done just that. Keep the faith and keep your eyes open as I did, and you will notice the things that you desire starting to come to you. Train yourself to imagine that which you want most. It can be as clear as if it were standing right in front of you or more general, like the mindset I just described. Keep your eyes open and your focus on what you truly desire.

By being focused on my dreams and open, I've found many amazing opportunities in my path throughout my life. Some provided great products, people, and training. Others provided the needed funds and interesting experiences with talented people. I also wanted a business opportunity that was in line with my desire to make a difference in the world. Many times, I've found just the right thing at the right time.

The opportunity with Elite Online Publishing came at such a perfect time and provided so much more than I could have imagined, but just what I'd been 'wanting'. I've received great training, the opportunity to work with two wonderful women and a flexible schedule that allowed me to work from anywhere, including Europe. All of that and I got paid to assist people in sharing their gifts with the world and making a difference in the lives of others through their books. I had expanded my ability to make a difference exponentially.

My intention is for this book to dramatically shorten the distance between where you are now and where you want to be. Through reading this book my intention is that you finally realize that you are currently where you've always 'wanted' to be. This concept will soon be explained as it may or may not seem that way currently.

The realization and acceptance of the fact that you are where you've been 'wanting' to be, is the secret to living a life that you love. Embracing gratitude, as well as developing the skill of creating dreams and goals that inspire you, will create the pathway. The practice of loving yourself and the art of acceptance are the keys. So put all of these together and you have the secret, the pathway and the keys to unlock a life you love.

In this book, I will share with you the story of my life. In each chapter, I will highlight lessons I've learned. Through these experiences and lessons I share, you will be better equipped to handle some of the challenges you face. In taking on the action steps at the end of each chapter, you will have the opportunity to take on your life. Get ready to create and embrace a life that you love right now.

The main purpose of this book is to, through illustration; show you how you too can love your life. There are several simple distinctions that will assist you.

1. Realize that where your focus goes, you go so watch out!
2. It starts with a way of being, not with what you do.
3. Cherish your moments and learn to experience them fully.
4. You can only truly be happy when you accept the way things are.
5. Your words create your world so be careful how you use them!.
6. You can either be right or be happy. You have to choose!
7. Let your light shine and share your gifts with the world
8. You are perfectly imperfect and so is your life!
   NOTE: You don't have to be perfect to be complete. I planned to get an editor for this book and I may for my future books as I know the value they bring. I may even choose to edit and re-release this book. However, this time I wanted to share myself, the real me. I got help from my friends and family and I love

them for it, but I love me the way I am and I wanted to share that with you, raw and unedited. So as you go through this book you might see some things you think to be a little off. Let's face it, aren't we all just a little bit off? I know I am. No-one is perfect. Keep reading for information on this point. If you find anything that brings up questions feel free to ask or to send feedback. I love questions and will happily look at including answers to yours in my next edition or as a post on my page Facebook.com/LoveYouToLifeCoach.

Answers to your questions could make a difference for people and that's the objective here. I truly appreciate the time you're taking to read this. It shows your commitment to yourself and your life. My email is Cory@ILoveMyselfSo.com.

9. In any moment, at any given time, you can reinvent you!
10. Look for and seize opportunities in all areas of your life.
11. Get out of your comfort zone to create an extraordinary life.
12. Remember the ABC's of life. Always Be Creating!
13. Your attitude determines your altitude.
14. Do more than just set your goals and forget them.
15. Celebrate your achievement when you reach a goal.
16. Create stepping stones to lift you up to reach your goals.
17. Take Action! Nothing happens until something or someone moves. I placed action steps at the end of each chapter so that you can immediately start taking action in your life. I suggest getting a journal to start these actions with. You also have a summary of all the lessons and action steps from every chapter at the end as a quick reference guide. The actions steps suggested in several chapters may take time to complete. I've created a workbook accompaniment for this book to make taking action easier. Feel free to keep reading and come back after you've finished reading to complete all of the action steps and refer back as life changes to update your goals dreams and plans. If you'd like to use either the journal or the workbook that go with this book you can find them by going to www.ILoveMyselfSo.com.

Consider for a moment how you would approach each choice you were faced with in life if you started by asking this question:

If I truly loved myself, what would I do in this moment?

I assure you that your actions would alter drastically for the good if you came from there each time you were faced with making a choice.

Let's dive right in and get started now, shall we?

To accomplish great things
we must not only act,
but also dream;
not only plan,
but also believe.

~ Anotole France

WHEN I LET GO OF WHAT I AM,
I BECOME WHAT
I MIGHT BE.

~ LAO TZU

SECTION ONE

Building a Strong Foundation

NOTHING IS IMPOSSIBLE,
THE WORD ITSELF SAYS 'I'M POSSIBLE!'

~ AUDREY HEPBURN

1

WHERE YOUR FOCUS GOES YOU GO

Ready for a bike ride around Pineview Lake
Eden, Utah

It's amazing how much a simple bike ride can teach you about focusing on what you want. I used to be afraid to go thru small spaces on a bike or in a car. This feeling stemmed from bike and car accidents in my past. Shortly after I started driving, I was headed out of my neighborhood and while exiting, I scooted my car over a bit to let a car into the subdivision from the main road. However, as I scooted over, I heard the fender of my huge Delta 88 scrape down the entire side of the cute little fiat parked in the no parking zone.   It was my first accident and it stuck with me.

Ever since then, I get nervous in tight spaces with any car I drive. I also had a few accidents on my bike. In one I was turning and my bike slipped out from under me leaving a little scar on my shoulder. In the other, I was going over a curb and my feet slipped off the pedals and my pelvic bone slammed into the corner of the handlebars. I swear that if I were a guy, I'd have been infertile from that because it hurt so badly.

These accidents combined to give me a fear that my handlebars were going to hit the sides of any tight spaces and I'd fall off and get hurt. I started focusing on the sides of any opening I went through. I'd get so scared that I would freeze up. When I thought I'd come close to hitting the sides I usually got off my bike to walk it through instead. It was no fun and really slowed me down. That was especially challenging when riding with friends. I choose to work through this when I moved to Utah. I lived right by a river parkway that had several gates flanked by two poles. I was committed to getting past this so I could enjoy my time out biking with friends.

When you're focused on what you *don't* want, even if you *don't* crash, you'll still end up stressed and stiff from what you put yourself thru. This is the same as placing your focus on the poles on either side as I did the first few times through. I got nervous and froze to the point that, if something did happen, I would have been too rigid to do anything about it. There's no room for a fluidity of motion when you're scared stiff.

I practiced going through these gates over and over until I could finally relax! If at first you don't succeed try and try again. Habits and automatic responses take time to retrain. It takes dedication and work to train or retrain your brain to focus on the positive or the goal. Some say practice makes perfect and others say perfect practice makes perfect. In my case, I was working to retrain my brain to focus on the goal versus the poles. I was also working to relax and enjoy the moment.

Your brain has been trained for years to focus on the negative and naturally uses the word *don't*. It's silly to expect to alter this overnight. You have to catch yourself in the act of focusing on the negative and stop yourself. It will take time and practice to retrain your brain. It may even take time to catch yourself in the act of saying *don't* since it's so ingrained. Just as it took me time to get comfortable riding through gates and driving in tight spaces, it took time to begin speaking in the affirmative. At the beginning of spring, after not riding my bike all winter, it still takes a few practice runs to get comfortable. Be kind to yourself and give yourself time to adjust.

Today I focus on the goal. I know that if I line my tire up with the center line, the gate is wide enough for a bike to ride thru. So... I'll be ok.

There are a few things needed here:
1. Focus on what you want.
2. Trust that the universe is set up to get you thru it safely.
3. Practice!

Note: Obviously you have to use common sense. You wouldn't take your bike through a gate only meant for pedestrians. However, if you've been through the gate before or seen others reach a goal you're striving for, you know it can be done.

It really is set up for you to win. All you have to do is focus on what you want and trust that things are set up to assist you in achieving your goals. The law of attraction calls to you what you're putting out into the world. When you're putting out negativity and resentment for things that you *don't* like or *don't* want, you're calling more of them into your life. The universe doesn't deal well with negativity. It's doesn't hear 'no' or 'not' when you think or speak those words. If you focus on what it is that you do *not* want, the universe only hears that you 'want' that. Since the universe is programmed to say yes, you then end up with what it heard you say that you 'want'. This is what I meant in the introduction when I said you are where you've been 'wanting' to be.

If you focus on the gate posts or poles and not the center line, you'll hit the poles every time. You'll run into the obstacles you are working so hard to avoid. In other words, if you focus on what you don't want you'll hit it every time. You'll call that same person into your life that you don't want. You'll lose that item you said you didn't want to lose. If you focus the centerline or goal on what you do want, then you're set. If you're grateful for the small things that do come your way, that gratitude and that focus bring more of the same into your life.

Start focusing on and channeling your energy into the things you do want. You will start to notice that you are stressing less and enjoying life more. It's all about shifting your focus. So next time you hear the word 'don't', in your mind or coming out of your mouth, I invite you to stop and change your focus. Instead, try saying, I want more of XYZ, whatever it may be.

For example:
In saying simple things like, 'I don't want to forget that appointment.' What the universe hears is, 'I do want to forget that appointment.' Simply rephrasing that to say, 'I'm going to remember that appointment.' will tell the universe that you want to remember that appointment. Another simple example would be saying, 'Don't slam the door.' What the universe hears is. 'Slam the door.' The universe simply says yes. So... whoever you just said that to will most likely slam the door because that's what they heard as well. If you were to instead say, please

close the door gently, the universe, as well as the person, will hear exactly what you want! So... they are inclined to do just that.

When you focus on what you want or where you want to go, you can get there more easily. Your handlebars clear the poles and you get thru the gate with ease, as in my earlier example. Then you get to celebrate hitting the center line, staying on course and attaining your goal. You're relaxed, happy and flowing with life versus fighting it. You end up energized instead of stressed. So you chose: celebrating and energized or stressed. Which way would you like to live life? I know for me it's celebrating and energized, so I'll focus on what I want because I know that then I'll be much closer to getting it!

Here's another story to illustrate further the importance of focusing on what you want. I spent the greater part of a summer in France and then traveling from Ireland down to Croatia, visiting a total of sixteen countries.

As I sat on the train from friend to friend, Liverpool to the Cotswolds, in England; I watched the beautiful countryside complete with tranquil ponds and creeks cutting through the lush green grass. There were sheep, cows, and cute cottages. I was reminded just how amazing it was that I was spending the summer in and around Europe! How lucky had I been in my life to meet such generous people who now allowed me to visit their neck of the woods and stay with them? How lucky was I to be to get to see how their life unfolded each day. Then I realized that it wasn't by luck, but rather by design that all of this came about.

Friendly faces greeted me as I got on the train asking polite questions. One offered Wi-Fi as they sat down across from me. We passed the time chatting about what brought us to the area and connecting on Facebook for the future. It really is true that life is a mirror. Not only do you find people like you, but you also find what you're looking for in life. This is why I focus on looking for positive, happy, and supportive people. It's also, I think, why I continue to find them? This amazes those not looking for the same in life. They are unaware that their focus could make all the difference.

Countless times I've talked to people who say that certain cities or areas are full of rude people and countless times I've been to those areas and found the opposite to be true. The worst is when they discount a country completely by saying that everybody is rude and uninviting. There are millions of people in thousands of cities all over the world. Not every single one of them could possibly be rude in any country, area or city.

When I moved to Salt Lake people said that I would find no welcome there, given that I wasn't Mormon. I assured them that wouldn't be the case and I was right. No matter what you're looking for, you'll find it. Remember, the universe wants to say yes. I was looking for happy, helpful, positive, and supportive people and I found them. What you put out, you get back. I put positivity out into the world and it came back to me tenfold in Utah, and everywhere else I've been in the U.S, as well as Australia, England, Ireland, France, and on and on. Everywhere I go, I find happy, positive, supportive people. I could probably count on one hand the people I've met who were anything but that.

Not only are you where you've been 'wanting' to be. You also have the things you've been telling the universe you want to have. You could also say you have arrived where you've been acting like you 'wanted' to go. Yet another version of this might be that you are now where your previous focus has led you. Where you place your focus and who you choose to 'be' will determine your outcomes in life. Whether you have been choosing these things consciously or unconsciously, the things you've said you wanted have come to you, both positive and negative.

Take a look at your life: the good, the bad and the ugly. Look to see what you have been focused on. Remember, what you focus on grows. So... let me ask you. Do you think you've said I *don't* want this or I *don't* want that a few times? Did you focus on how you looked, in a *negative* context? Did you relate to the people around you with *complaints*, focused on the things you *didn't* like about them or with compliments, focused on the amazing qualities they possess. Do you have more of the things you *don't* want or *don't* like than things you *do* want?

I can tell you that I spent seven years losing focus. I fell out of balance. I was focusing on my job and getting out of debt more than my health and happiness. I was not focused on my physical well being. After that long, it took a serious reboot or 'brainwashing' to kick the stinkin' thinkin' to the curb. I had certainly started having a lot more of the negative in my words and in my life. I forgot who I was so to speak and it had an impact in several areas of my life. My finances were in great shape, but that doesn't create a happy life. Balance creates a happy life. Finances are important, but what good would all the money in the world do if you didn't have your health and happiness? None, right? Balance is essential. Take time for you. Without self-care, we get burnt out quickly. Taking time to nourish the body, mind, and spirit is the key. That's a whole book in and of itself though. Stay tuned.

No book, seminar, class, coaching or any amount of self-help work will work unless you turn the lessons into habits so strong that you naturally do them. Let me say that I have taken so many of these that if they were the answer, I'd be perfect. I've also read so many great books that if they were the answer I'd always do the right things. It takes you continuing to learn, grow and focus on the positive. It takes you creating a future that inspires you to be the person it will take to get there. It takes you stepping into that future every day when you wake up, every time you make a choice. It takes living into that future you created in every breath. In short, it takes you focusing on what you truly want!

Do you have wonderful people in your life? Are you doing what you've always 'wanted' to do? Are you where you've said you 'wanted' to be? I assert that you are. By virtue of that fact that you may have accidentally said you *didn't* want many of these things. However, the universe only heard the 'want' part and unfortunately skipped over the word *didn't*.

If you focus on any belief long enough, the law of attraction will give you evidence for that belief. And it has no self-interest. So if you believe that all this law of attraction stuff is nonsense, you'll get evidence for that belief. That doesn't mean either belief for or against it is right. But no one can prove either. Either focus will bring evidence for the belief you focus on. You will find lots of evidence for your argument to either end. You can be righteous, therefore, about either, in fact, any belief. Being righteous can inhibit happiness especially when your focus is on negative facts or limiting beliefs.

Even if the negative facts are true, for example, someone is mean or rude. Focussing on that fact gives you nothing positive in life. You can choose to focus on their positive qualities, like their intelligence or positive impacts they may have in any situation. This focus can help you relate to people in general as well as relieve some of the struggle, stress or frustration in any relationship. Focusing on finding the good in people will reap benefits well beyond your peace of mind and a lack of negativity and stress in your life. That positive focus can actually call more of the good out in that person, having a positive impact on the world around them, not just your life.

You really do find what you're looking for. So... start focusing on and looking for the good in the world, in people and in yourself! Start speaking in the affirmative. Affirming what you want allows the universe to start saying yes to that which you truly desire.

Life Lessons:

1. What you focus on grows. So... Create something amazing to focus on. Focus on things you want to grow and multiply.
2. Where your focus goes, you go. So... Set goals that focus you in the direction you want to go.
3. What you focus on, you'll create. So... Focus on and even dream about what you want to create.
4. What you look for, you'll find. So... Search for the things you want to find in life. Search for the good in people and the world around you.
5. Focus solely on the positive to grow the positive things in your life.
    a. Be grateful for what you're happy you have and you'll get more of those positive things in your life.
    b. Focus on things you don't like or want and you'll get more of those.
    c. So... Choose to focus on the positive.
6. Focusing on taking care of you is as important as any other goal.
7. So... Focus on showing yourself, love.

Action Steps:

1. Create a list of things that light you up, things you love. Here's an example of some things I love: sunsets, singing, dancing, hiking, travelling, and playing cards with friends and family.
2. Create a list of the monetary or physical goals you are working towards. Here are a few of mine to get you started: healthy living, great relationships, passive income sufficient to travel and making a difference in the world.
3. What will having those things provide for your life?
4. What is your vision of a perfect life?
5. What is your vision of a perfect world?
6. Describe your perfect relationship?
7. Describe your perfect day?
8. Let's start creating them!

I ATTRACT TO MY LIFE WHATEVER I GIVE MY
ATTENTION, ENERGY AND FOCUS TO,
WHETHER POSITIVE OR NEGATIVE.

~ MICHAEL LOSIER

~~~~~~~

WHERE YOUR FOCUS GOES, ENERGY FLOWS.

~ TONY ROBBINS

THINKING

IF YOU THINK YOU ARE BEATEN, YOU ARE
IF YOU THINK YOU DARE NOT, YOU DON'T,
IF YOU LIKE TO WIN, BUT YOU THINK YOU CAN'T
IT IS ALMOST CERTAIN YOU WON'T.

IF YOU THINK YOU'LL LOSE, YOU'RE LOST
FOR OUT OF THE WORLD WE FIND,
SUCCESS BEGINS WITH A FELLOW'S WILL
IT'S ALL IN THE STATE OF MIND.

IF YOU THINK YOU ARE OUTCLASSED, YOU ARE
YOU'VE GOT TO THINK HIGH TO RISE,
YOU'VE GOT TO BE SURE OF YOURSELF BEFORE
YOU CAN EVER WIN A PRIZE.

LIFE'S BATTLES DON'T ALWAYS GO
TO THE STRONGER OR FASTER MAN,
BUT SOON OR LATE THE MAN WHO WINS
IS THE MAN WHO THINKS HE CAN!

WHERE YOUR FOCUS GOES, YOU GO.
SO WATCH OUT!

~ CORY JENKINS

2

WHO WOULD YOU HAVE TO BE?

In one of my favorite zen places
Silver Lake, Utah

Who would you have to be to have the life of your dreams? Would you have to be enthusiastic, charismatic, passionate, inspirational, caring, loving, open, joyful, grateful, accepting, free or something entirely different? Are you 'being' that person now?

Consider for a moment that what you have now is a reflection of who you are 'being' and in order to have something different you have to 'be' someone different. Notice that I didn't say become, but rather 'be' someone different. You don't have to wait to become something more, better or different. You can 'be' the person you want to 'be' today. That will most likely mean getting out of your comfort zone, far, far out of that comfort zone.

In the next section you will be asked to list several things you long for in life. You will also make a list of the people who have qualities that you admire as well as the results they have. For now, take a moment to pause and think about people you've met who have the things you desire. I am going to ask you to describe them in ways of being. Are they caring? Are they generous? Do they show gratitude for the things in their life? I assert that they got the results you long for by 'being' a person that calls those things into their life.

It all starts with 'being'. You may describe them as 'being' grateful, loving, generous or enthusiastic. Now, look to identify the actions they took that made you think they were that way. Perhaps they volunteered, which you experienced as a generous or loving action.

The question to ask yourself, at any given moment is: What actions would a generous, loving, enthusiastic, 'fill in the blank' person take in this moment toward that result? Come from there. If you desire to have those results, choose to 'be' a person that attracts them. Then you'll naturally be called to 'do' the things consistent with 'being' that person. When you come from 'being' loving, your thoughts will naturally lead you to take loving actions. It's in this way that you start calling into your life the things you want to 'have.' This new way that you are now 'being', then gives you the actions to take or what to 'do'. Your actions then give you your results or what you 'have' in life.

Some might refer to this as faking it till you make it. However, when you focus on coming from a new way of being, then the actions you take now have purpose behind them.

In sales, I was taught to match and mirror people. However, the purpose behind this was to sell to someone. By mirroring the client you make yourself more familiar and they naturally feel more comfortable around you. When you take it from simply matching and mirroring to stepping into their shoes, and truly 'being' with them, then your purpose becomes doing what best serves them. When you add the concept of 'being' to it, it becomes so much more powerful and impactful for both parties. People can feel the shift and they become naturally more comfortable around you. It's not a show anymore that's simply done in order to sell.

Several of my clients became close friends because I came from caring about them and their needs versus a fake sales gimmick. You too can use this in a positive way to truly 'be' the person you want to 'be' right now. You don't have to wait till someday. You get to be that powerful, inspiring, 'fill in the blank' person now.

The attitude of gratitude could be used as an example. I've noticed that when I've physically thought, 'How can I express my gratitude for the people, events and things in my life?' I've wanted to do this like my friends who do it so eloquently. How can I show my appreciation for the generosities I've experienced from friends or the amazing gifts the universe has given me? It's when I come from a mindset of simply 'being' grateful that the answers to these questions simply flow.

I can easily overlook gifts and generous acts when I'm not in the moment and not paying attention. I can easily get caught up in something else and forget who I 'am'. It's then that I forget to 'be' grateful and therefore forget to take any actions to show my gratitude. I can forget to 'be' many amazing things that I would normally choose to 'be' when I'm in the moment. You've heard people refer to forgetting themselves. They may overstep some boundary they've created and say something inappropriate. The same goes when you forget yourself. You forget the way of 'being' that you created that allows the actions to flow that will give you everything you want in life.

One of my best friends, we'll call her Ginger, shared a story with me about being happy. One day, while driving down the street, she noticed a man next to her at a stoplight rocking out and dancing to whatever music was playing in his car. We've all had that experience, right? She shared with me that in that moment she thought 'Man! I need to be happy like that guy.'

Now when she's frustrated or down, she remembers that guy rocking out in his car. She remembers that she too can simply choose to 'be' happy. She may put on some music to get into the right mindset. However, sometimes a simple memory or thought can assist you in triggering a way of being that inspires you. It could be a memory of your favorite person 'being' loving towards you or someone else. Maybe it's an iconic figure in your life that was inspirational, or it could be someone in history that you saw as charismatic. It could also quite simply be a person you saw for just an instant, like my friend, that left a lasting impression.

We all experience people in different ways. For you, the man rocking out in his car beside you might symbolize being free and not caring what others think. Others may see him as both free and happy and still others could see something totally different in that moment. Find your own examples and triggers that work for you and inspire you to be the way you desire to be. The actions will fall into place when you come from this new mindset.

When you come from a state of 'being' that reflects the true person you want to share with the world, the actions flow naturally to give you the results that you desire.

Life Lessons:

1. It all starts with a way of 'being'.
2. The best feeling is when you own your new way of being.
3. When you feel a new way of being from your heart; you have it.
4. 'Being' starts with the heart.
5. Think: Who would I have to 'be' to 'have' everything I want?
6. Your way of 'being' gives you the actions to 'do'.
7. Your 'doing' gives you the results you want in life or what you 'have'.
8. 'Be' the 'you', you've always wanted to 'be' and you'll begin to 'do' the things necessary to 'have' what you've always wanted.
9. Think - Be, Do, Have.
10. You Be You, The World Will Adjust!

Action Steps:

1. Invent a new way of being to live and take action from.
   a. The answer to the question "Who are you?" always starts with I am... not I'm becoming or I want to be. Just a simple declaration... I am... 'fill in the blank.' You are speaking it into existence. For Example: Since learning this technique, I have created several new ways of being
      i. Before my marriage I created - I am free, open, playful and passionate.
      ii. Recently, while working on getting back to my healthy self, I created - I am a beautiful, loving, healing, passionate woman.
   b. Finding a way to love your life now is as important as creating things to love about your life. Look back at all the lists you made in the last chapter as you answer the following questions. As you delve into this book, come back and add to or alter your answers as you create and embrace new areas of your life as well as new dreams and goals. Answer the following questions in your journal or workbook:
      i. Who would I have to 'be' to love my life now?

      ii.   What type of person would it take to create the results I am now focused on and truly want in my life?

      iii.   How would it feel to have what I want?

      iv.   How would this person, a.k.a. me, act if I had attained my goals?

      v.   What ways of being will I now create for myself?

      vi.   So... Who Am I?

      vii.   What actions would this person, a.k.a. me, naturally take?

2. Each morning take a moment to close your eyes and imagine yourself already having the results you want in life.

3. Throughout the day as you are faced with choices as to what actions to take in your life, ask yourself silently or out loud: What would a (insert your inspiring way of being here) do? For Example: What would a free, open, playful and passionate person do right now in this situation?

    a. It's ok to imagine what someone else would do until you start imagining yourself doing these things.

    b. Then think of/imagine yourself doing the same thing.

    c. Once you have it in mind, take the actions you see needed coming from your new way of being.

    d. It would be beneficial to watch videos of people doing what it is you plan to do if that applies. You may also want to find pictures on the internet to post on your vision board. There are several guides to assist you with these actions. Visualization and vision board creation are also covered in my Love you to Life Course.

4. Choose an action item from your list that you are committed to take on consistently from your new way of being, towards your desired results for at least the next 21 days. (It takes 21 days to build a habit) Go for it!

5. The easiest way to take this on will be to take on one habit to support your new way of being a month. You can go faster if you like and take on a new one every 21 days or even sooner. However, it's nice to give yourself time to cement in place your new habits and ways of being.

6. Be sure to write down the habits you plan to cultivate, the actions that will have you take and the results you expect to create through forming each new habit. Again you can use your own journal or purchase the journal and/or workbook that go with this book. The Journal has inspirational quotes and thought-provoking questions to help you along your journey. The workbook has every question here with room to write out your answers.

7. www.ILoveMyselfSo.com will direct you to the Amazon Page with the I Love Myself So Quotes & Questions Journal as well as the workbook so you can continually track your results for new projects and habits. You will want to repeat this process throughout your life as your goals and dreams are realized and you continue to create new ones to achieve.

ALWAYS BE A FIRST RATE VERSION OF
YOURSELF & NOT A SECOND RATE
VERSION OF SOMEONE ELSE

~ JUDY GARLAND

~~~~~~~

BE YOURSELF;
EVERYONE ELSE IS ALREADY TAKEN

~ OSCAR WILDE

~~~~~~~

I AM NOT A PRODUCT OF MY
CIRCUMSTANCES.
I AM A PRODUCT OF MY DECISIONS.

~ STEPHEN COVEY

3

ENJOY EVERY MOMENT

Hotel ZaDar - Poolside breakfast
Zadar, Croatia

While on a trip through Europe, I stopped in Croatia following the advice of friends and my gut. In my second city there, I arrived to find my favorite hostel of the whole trip. It had a large bed, a pool, and an amazing breakfast. I decided to stay another night again following my gut. Both nights I had only two roommates vs. four. Bonus! They were also all hot men! Double Bonus!

When I woke up the next morning, I was able to, enjoy the pool after a long leisurely breakfast as see above and then rent a bike and take a nice ride. After I stopped by the bus station to find the route to Krka National Park for the following day, I headed to the beach to find a place to relax. I planned to fully enjoy and take in this beautiful day and gorgeous city. I found the perfect place with an outstanding view of the ocean and the most delicious beet, arugula, pine nut and feta salad. I settled in to relax and reflect. That's when I realized that I had arrived at the perfect place, time and moment.

As I watching all the beautiful people walk by, it was amazing realizing how beautiful everyone was in their own unique way with their varying types of bathing suits and body styles. I took off my dress and relaxed in my own bathing suit after lunch, wishing that I had decided on a bikini so that I could take full advantage of the sun. It was at that moment that I chose to go buy one in this town or the next.

Leaving my purse with the waiter, I headed off to stroll down the beach and jump in the water. I had chosen my moment in the sun well and truly enjoyed every second. After relaxing a while longer back at my table, I hopped on my bike to go further explore the old town of Zadar. I found a bikini that I really liked and I asked the shopkeeper to set it aside so I could consider it. I then took off on my little bike to ride around the ruins downtown and capture the beauty in photo souvenirs. I realized, at some point that I had found the perfect bikini. So... I went back, bought it and wore it the next day and every opportunity thereafter! I still love it!

Choose to be present in the moment. When you are worrying about the future or fretting about the past you are living in the future or the past. Living in the now and going with the flow will give you access to loving your life. So... go with the Flow

Cory in new bikini with new friend Djana Fahry -Author 'The Soul Trek'
Le Plage Mala- Cap d'Ail- Côte d-Azur, France

Life Lessons:

1. Be present.
2. Enjoy every moment.
3. Experience your moments your way.
4. Swim with the current versus upstream. Go with the flow of life.
5. Hit the pause button and take your time. Soak in every second.

Action Steps:

1. Take time out in the evening to take note of a beautiful moment

you experienced throughout your day. As you begin to do this each night you may find that you begin to notice the moments as they happen versus having to reflect back to remember them. Write down a few you remember.

2. Begin to plan out moments like the day I described above. These moments will allow you to practice being present and truly enjoying each second. Write out a few examples of moments you can imagine creating for yourself to enjoy.

3. Practice makes perfect. So... keep practicing these until you start to notice when you aren't present. Being present is one of the keys to loving your life. When you are stuck in regret about the past or worry about the future you are not able to enjoy the gift that being present provides. As you begin to create them, make note of the moments where you experience being fully present to your life. How did it feel? What did that create for you and those around you? Begin to journal about these moments ongoingly. The 'I Love Myself So... Quotes and Questions Journal' can help inspire you to create and capture these moments daily. This will help you remember that life is a gift.

THE CLOCK IS RUNNING. MAKE THE MOST
OF TODAY. TIME WAITS FOR NO MAN.
YESTERDAY IS HISTORY. TOMORROW IS A
MYSTERY. TODAY IS A GIFT. THAT'S WHY
IT IS CALLED THE PRESENT.

~ALICE MORSE EARLE
~SUN DIALS AND ROSES OF YESTERDAY

~~~~~~

DOES ANYONE EVER REALIZE LIFE WHILE
THEY LIVE IT...EVERY, EVERY MINUTE?

~ EMILY
~ THORNTON WILDER'S ~ OUR TOWN

LIFE IS A JOURNEY,
NOT A DESTINATION.

~ RALPH WALDO EMERSON

~~~~~~~

GIVE EVERY DAY
THE CHANCE TO BECOME
THE MOST BEAUTIFUL
OF YOUR LIFE.

~ MARK TWAIN

4

ACCEPT WHAT IS

**My last picture with the necklace my mom gave me.
Davis County Gala Night - Layton, Utah**

When it looks like everything's is going wrong, change your perspective and accept that everything happens for a reason. Some people say 'Things don't just happen, they happen just.' Just, in this sense, means they are fair and or have a reason behind them. I love this saying because it implies the underlying meaning that everything happens for a reason. You can also add to it and say things happen just right. Just right can mean that things happen at just the right moment or in just the right way to accomplish some needed outcome. Many things happen at just the right time to teach a lesson, others to open a new door or simply open your eyes. Once such lesson came at, what some could say was just the right time to provide something needed in my life.

I had just purchased a bedroom set for the guest bedroom to house my family for Thanksgiving. I was looking into renting the room out after they left. I spoke to a possible renter who was in a seemingly bad way that weekend. My big heart couldn't leave him out in the cold, so against my better judgment, I took him in for the weekend. (Note: Follow your gut. It's usually right. However, I guess it was my time to be reminded of this lesson.)

I let him stay for the weekend. He promised to pay the first and last month's rent on Monday. I saw several holes in his story so when he started trying to convince me that the sale of his business was having challenges the next morning, I was done. He called his 'dad' and had a conversation within earshot about the lawyer selling the business needing a payment that day to finish the paperwork by Monday. I knew he was just trying to get me to offer up the money. I told him that no lawyer was going to request money on a Saturday for any reason and recommended he call back his dad and find out the real story. Then I politely wished him good luck and stepped away to make a call. It goes on, but what a story! He then said he was going for a walk and asked if I could close the garage door after him. I thought, *the garage?!?* I told him to go out the front door and he gave me the lame excuse that he'd get lost that way since we'd come in the back.

If I hadn't been on the phone in the middle of the conversation I would have gotten up to see what was up, but I was preoccupied and annoyed by him at this point so I sent him out the front door and asked when he'd be back. He said he had to go close the garage door which confused me then said he'd be back in 10-15 minutes, but then text in a bit saying his friend had picked him up to go get some of his things. He gave me a few even more ludicrous excuses later in the day as to why he wasn't yet returning.

He had folded my clothes and put them nicely on my bed since we'd done a load of laundry together. I remember thinking, *At least he was polite.* Later that night a little voice stopped me while passing my dresser to look in a jewelry box. Almost everything was gone. What I had missed earlier is that he'd dropped his bag with my jewelry in it out the back door so I couldn't see he was leaving. That's why he was trying to exit that way. That's explained *the garage?!?* (Note: Lock away your valuables when renting out your spare room.) I went to the police but they didn't seem to be able to find anything. In my defense, I learned from the police that he was a professional con man who wrote a book on his escapades. However, his other marks must have been completely stupid if they bought dad act, but he still got something out of me. At last count, I'd lost over $5000 worth of jewelry. (Note: Always do background checks and get a down payment before allowing a rental candidate to stay in your home.)

I looked for it at a few pawn shops over the next couple months and then gave up. My insurance only covered $1500 worth of jewelry without the proper rider (Note: Check your coverage if you have expensive jewelry) The insurance check ironically came in at a time when I was due to pay off one of my low-interest rate credit cards from the condo purchase I'd had to make on credit card. Even more ironic is that the amount I still owed was exactly $1500. I had said to myself this money is going to show up.

Be careful what and how you wish for things. They may show up in quite random ways otherwise. I've been amazed at how things have manifested in my life, but sometimes the details aren't quite spot on. I was going to have to borrow that $1500, but instead, it was delivered just in time to pay off the loan.

I chose not to pursue a case against this person and I've chosen not to pursue cases or go after people for money several times. I have chosen to focus on the positives in life. Going after any of these people for money or damages would require my time and attention. It would also cause stress and frustration. What is your time worth to you? What is your health worth? What is your peace of mind worth? I chose to value myself and these over any money I may have recaptured. I am worth way more than a few thousand dollars. So... I also chose to stay positive. I am confident that some of the people, who I let out of sticky financial situations worth $2,000, $3,000 and even once $3,500, may have needed the money more than I did. It also wasn't worth my time to chase after a few thousand dollars. Your time and your peace of mind are worth much more! Being right about principle and having a few thousand dollars won't make you happy if you aren't already able to be happy without it.

Some would say I follow the statement, 'Let go and let God.' This philosophy has saved me from allowing other people or circumstances to have a negative impact on my life.

Accepting what is so you can move on isn't a perfect science. It takes practice and a commitment to creating a life that works for you. It is quite necessary if you want to love your life. Being stuck in what's wrong or focusing on what doesn't work, simply doesn't work. You will find that letting go of expectations and how you think things 'should be' is a necessity when it comes to living a life you love. Letting go allows you to go with the flow of life, to experience and enjoy every moment. It allows you to get wrapped up in the beauty of awe-inspiring moments in life, like finding your rings after having thought they were lost to you forever.

Fast forward a year and I'd almost put the incident out of my mind. I decided to stroll along Ogden's 25th to see what was new and enjoy a bit a window shopping when I passed by a pawn shop and my jewelry came to mind. Even though I knew it had been a year, something was pulling me towards the door. I felt a strong urge to go inside and though I didn't see any jewelry at first, for some reason, I kept walking. I went all the way to the back and there in front of me, below the glass, sat the promise ring my first boyfriend had given me as well as a ring that my mom had given me to go with the necklace in the picture above. I couldn't believe it!!!

I went to the police the next day and they were able to reclaim my rings. The shop had already sold the other items, but I was in ecstatic that I'd found the rings. I still had the earrings that go with the amethyst set my mom gave me. Truth be told I'd only worn any of these pieces a few times in the past 10-20 years so $1500 was more useful than having the jewelry. I thought of this and several other things when I realized they were gone in getting over the sting of the loss. Focussing on the silver lining and the positives will help you get through many things. Will I miss them every once in a while? Yes. Am I lost without them? Definitely not... It's just stuff. Stuff is far less important than my happiness. Letting go of frustration allowed me to get back to loving my life. That means way more to me than material items.

Start letting go and going with the flow of life. Love your life just the way it is and just the way it's not. Wanting life to be something else only leads to frustration and disappointment. Start loving you just the way you are and just the way you're not. Love you where you are now, don't wait until you or your life are more, better or different. Start appreciating the little things you have now. Let go of the trivial things that are currently taking up that space in your brain. Create space needed to notice these little things as tiny miracles.

Notes:

1. Follow your gut. It's usually right.
2. Sometimes it just your time to be reminded of a lesson.
3. Check insurance coverages/riders if you have expensive jewelry.
4. You may want to lock away your valuables when renting out your spare room to a person you don't fully know yet.
5. You may want to hire a property manager if you have rentals. They are a more impersonal way to approach rental ownership. The cost can save you stress, frustration and time. However, I love knowing my tenants. However I now always Do Background Checks and get a down payment before allowing a rental candidate to stay in any of my properties and especially my own home. In several cases, I trusted my gut and chose renters who may not have looked great on paper with credit checks, but were perfect in real life. In fact, some who traditional evaluations would say looked the worst, turned out to be the best! Do your homework and get training or one on one coaching

if you plan to purchase and/or manage investment properties.

Life lessons:

1. Accept what is.
2. Expect Miracles.
3. Let go to let the miracles flow!
4. Stuff is far less important than happiness.
5. Things don't just happen, they happen just right.
6. Let karma do its work so you are free to enjoy your life.
7. Embrace the storms of life and learn to dance in the rain.
8. Letting go of any negative things currently taking up space in your mind will allow space for you to start appreciating the little things that make life beautiful.
9. Look for the empowering reasons, amazing lessons or opportunities provided when 'seemingly' bad things happened.

Action Steps:

1. You can now look back at things that have frustrated you in the past that you haven't let go of in a new light. Also, when you start to get frustrated in life, stop and think before you act: Use these steps for future as well as past frustrations you have in life.
   a. What actually happened?
   b. What good can getting frustrated accomplish?
   c. What negative consequences will my frustration have?
   d. What responsibility do I need to take in this situation?
      i. Did my actions in part or I full cause this?
      ii. Did I think of what the other person might have been going through in the situation? If so, how did I? If not, how can I in the future?
   e. What are the positive takeaways here?
      i. What can I do differently in the future?
      ii. What lessons can I learn here?
      iii. What good came out of it?
   f. How can I now reframe this incident in a positive light?

LIFE ISN'T ABOUT WAITING FOR THE STORMS TO PASS … IT'S ABOUT LEARNING TO DANCE IN THE RAIN.

~ VIVIAN GREENE

~~~~~~~

EACH PLAYER MUST ACCEPT THE CARDS LIFE DEALS HIM OR HER: BUT ONCE THEY ARE IN HAND, HE OR SHE ALONE MUST DECIDE HOW TO PLAY THE CARDS IN ORDER TO WIN THE GAME.

~ VOLTAIRE

ONCE WE ACCEPT OUR LIMITS WE GO
BEYOND THEM.

~ ALBERT EINSTEIN

~~~~~~~

TO COMPLAIN IS ALWAYS NONACCEPTANCE
OF WHAT IS. IT INVARIABLY CARRIES AN
UNCONSCIOUS NEGATIVE CHARGE. WHEN YOU
COMPLAIN, YOU MAKE YOURSELF INTO A
VICTIM. WHEN YOU SPEAK OUT, YOU ARE IN
YOUR POWER. SO CHANGE THE SITUATION BY
TAKING ACTION OR BY SPEAKING OUT IF
NECESSARY OR POSSIBLE; LEAVE THE SITUATION
OR ACCEPT IT. ALL ELSE IS MADNESS.

~ ECKHART TOLLE

5

W O R D S   A R E   K E Y S   T O
U N L O C K   Y O U R   D R E A M S

Sunset through a 'Key' hole in a bridge railing
Paris, France

Words can be the windows or barriers to new and amazing worlds. The key lies in either choosing your words wisely or carelessly throwing around your words as if they are worthless. Your words create your world. Everything counts! Including and especially the words you say to yourself inside your head that only you can hear. These words can actually matter the most. They set the tone for your life and all of the interactions you have. Those words said only for you to hear are felt in every interaction and seen in every reaction from the people in your life.

It is true that you can't love anything till you love yourself. The words you say either give love or take it away. They give you amazing experiences or frustration and disappointments. You experience everyone in your life through the words you use to describe them and your interactions with them.

We touched on speaking in positive terms when speaking about things you desire. This was in order to use the law of attraction. When you say don't or do not, the universe only hears the do. It skips over the word not, as it deals only in the affirmative. You can also use the law of attraction with people in your life. You can literally speak into existence the person you want to show up in your life. It may be the same person that was already there but now begins to show up differently by virtue of the way you're speaking. Become a good finder with the people in your life and you'll start to see more and more good in them. Not just because you're looking for it but because by virtue of looking for it, you begin to speak it into existence. Praise and appreciate the good and you'll get more of it from those in your life. Including yourself. We can be our own worst critic or strongest advocate. It's so important to pay attention to what the little voice in your head is saying to you day in and day out. Your subconscious can be for or against you, but you must train it in the art of working for you. We will touch on this in several chapters in many different ways, because it is the single most important thing in life! You can only go as high or as far as you believe you can!

This works with everything in your life. Not just people and things but circumstances and moments. I realized when I had rented out my house and was leaving for Europe I had four homes to rent but five rentals because I had both bedrooms in my current home rented separately. I set a goal to have five rentals and I had technically achieved it. I also set a goal to buy a house every one to three years. In this way, I could live in them to season the loan and get the best rate. My last goal was five houses within fifteen years. At the time of writing this, I still had a few years on that goal and a plan in place for its attainment. I discuss this more in section two when I get into the story of my life.

Words are the windows to creation. You must be careful in all that you say. Be clear and positive in your speaking. You create your experience of the world through the words you use to describe it and your results through the words you use to describe them! Start focusing on loving your life and making your dreams a reality. Then you will suddenly and continually find as well as create more to love.

Life Lessons:

1. Your words create your world.
2. Your words can be windows or barricades to your dreams.
3. Your words can give you more of what you want or more of what you are trying to avoid. You choose in the words you use.
   a. Use your words to praise and appreciate what you love and want in your life and you'll get more of it.
   b. Use your words to condemn and complain about what you dislike or detest in life and you'll get more of that.

Action Steps:

1. Write down everything you love in and about your life.
2. Write down everything you love about your body, mind, and spirit.
3. Write down all the words you could use and every action you could take to show yourself, love.
4. Write down the word and actions you could use to show love to those in your life.
5. Start taking those actions and saying those things and watch the love in your life grow exponentially.
6. Speak with the intention to create what you want. Start calling your desires to you. You will begin to see them materialize.
7. Remember to be grateful for all that you receive and create.

WHATEVER THE MIND CAN
CONCEIVE AND BELIEVE,
IT CAN ACHIEVE.

~ NAPOLEON HILL

6

BE RIGHT OR BE HAPPY

Trying too hard to 'Be Right' then letting go and 'Being Happy'
Cliffs of Moher- Co. Clare, Ireland

If you are always focused on 'getting it right,' you'll always be worried, stressed, and afraid. You'll never get out of your comfort zone and try new things for fear that you won't 'do it right.' When my life becomes about doing everything right or having to be right all the time, it ceases to be fun. It's usually not pleasant to be around somebody who insists on being right all the time. It's also not fun to be around somebody who's trying to be perfect all the time. They're usually stressed out and easily frustrated.

When you can let go of 'being right' and choose to have stress free and fun people around you, you get to experience a relaxed fun atmosphere. It's really a great place to be when you can go with the flow and allow things to just be the way they are.

I notice that I feel more stressed when I get around people that have to 'direct traffic,' as I call it. There's no way for me to feel free to relax and go with the flow. I also notice that I become more controlling myself. When I slip into these old ways of being I don't always notice it till later. Unfortunately, this can mean I've already said or done something that lowers the energy in the room or negatively impacts other people's lives in some way.

I am by far not perfect and my best moments come when I accept and let go of trying to be perfect or 'right.' That's when I have the opportunity to learn from life and others who may have something insightful to offer in whatever situation I find myself. It's funny how smart the people around you become when you start listening for their greatness.

Sometimes the hardest thing to do is to be quiet when you think you have the answer, especially when you're someone who's been trying to prove you're not 'stupid' for over twenty years. Needing to have the right answer and proving I'm smart has been one of my biggest challenges. I still slip into that mindset when I'm not paying attention and in situations that trigger that response. I believe that everyone has experienced that feeling.

When it becomes a battle of the 'rights' and you find yourself arguing as to who's right and who's wrong; nobody wins. Everyone is left feeling frustrated. However, some of my best lessons have come when I was paying attention and could feel the frustration rise. Realizing it in that moment or even just after, I have been able to let go of being right and thereby relax and enjoy the situation.

You are who you hang around. Some people say habits can be hereditary. I say habits are 'hangingarounditary.' Sometimes it takes work to train myself out of habits after spending time with certain people. If I know they have a habit that doesn't work for me, I can use time with them as a learning moment. Sometimes the best teachers in life are those that serve as a mirror to reflect something about ourselves that causes challenges in our lives. They can mirror this habit back to us to show how it makes us feel and react. If we notice this in the moment or even after, it can teach us how to manage that habit in ourselves. We can use it to eliminate disempowering habits.

I come from a family of strong women who are, as my mother would say, 'not always right but seldom uncertain.' In my first position as a sales manager in hotels, I worked with a lady at the front desk that was a great mirror for me. We would stop each other whenever it worked for us and ask for help with something, regardless of what the other person was in the middle of doing. Instead of choosing to wait until I knew she had time, I would justify my action saying to myself, *she does the same thing.* I chose not to acknowledge that it was just as frustrating for her as it was for me. It turned into a battle of paybacks.

After a few challenges, I chose to sit down with her and have a straight conversation. I listened to find out how she felt. When she could see my commitment to making our relationship work and I acknowledged what a difference she made in the ease of my work life we got past our frustrations. We became each other's biggest support at work and, after that conversation, loved working together. Notice I said after a few challenges because it can take time to admit that you could be part of the problem and that you can be the one to make a difference.

Sometimes you can work with the person, as in my case, but other times the work is done solely on your side. You can single-handedly change any relationship. You get to stop making them wrong and accept the way they are as well as the way they aren't. We talked about accepting what is as it relates to circumstances. This also includes the people in your life. When life becomes about making someone wrong or fixing them because you feel something is wrong with them then you've given away control of your happiness. You are in effect saying that unless they change, you won't be happy around them. Your happiness becomes tied to them taking some action and you lose control. When you accept 'what is' about someone, you allow them to be who they are. You can figure out how to alter your actions and reactions to them as they are versus changing them. Your happiness is then back in your control.

Take a look at your life and your most challenging relationships. What do they do that frustrates you so? Now look in your life with an open honest eye and see if you ever do the same sorts of things? Are they a mirror for you? Do they show you the qualities in yourself that you'd like to let go of or replace with empowering ways of being? Use this to your advantage. Practice being this new way around them and you'll notice that life becomes easier around them. Also, note that only you had to choose to make the difference. You get to choose a new way of being around them so you can enjoy your life and your time with them just the way they are.

You may now realize and can be grateful they uncovered a part of you that you didn't realize affected others in a negative way. These interactions can now be seen as opportunities for growth. Sometimes challenges and challenging people are just blessings in disguise.

The first step is noticing where you have been stressed out, frustrated, exhausted or anything else that doesn't work in your life. Think of what you've been doing that may have caused that feeling; what you've been doing that doesn't work. The next step is to notice when you begin doing the things that you've identified don't work. Once you identify what causes these upsets, you can begin choosing a different way of being in those situations. The final step is to start choosing different actions. These new actions will cause a difference in your results and allow you to be happy versus just 'being right.'

Warning: Possible Pitfall:
You may be tempted to 'should' on yourself. I invite you to fight this urge.

When you 'should' on yourself, no one wins. 'Shoulding' on yourself looks like this. Darn it, I 'should've' done this or I 'should've' done that. That is living in the past which you cannot change. It's much more empowering to look towards the future. Another way to frame this might be, '*Wow, I could have done it this way and then maybe this may have happened. Maybe I'll try that next time.*' Reflection can definitely be a positive thing. It's when judgment about your actions creeps in that you must beware. Judgment can be debilitating. It can rob you of the opportunity to learn valuable lessons from your actions and experiences.

There is no right or wrong; only 'what is.' Whatever is actually happening will be either working or not working. If it's not working you get to choose if you want to do something about it. If it's working you can simply roll with it or choose to improve on it if you so desire.

Life lessons:

1. You can either 'be right' or 'be happy.'
2. Accept the people in your life the way they are.
3. Learn to be quiet and listen for other people's greatness.
4. You can improve any relationship by altering only your actions.
5. Your most challenging person can bless you with your biggest lesson.
6. You are who you hang around. Some habits are 'hangingarounditary.'
7. 'Shoulding' on yourself accomplishes nothing but creating regrets.

Action steps:
Journal on the following topics:

1. Write down all of the times you feel mentally or physically exhausted, anxious, stressed and/or frustrated.
   a. Identification is the first step.
   b. Frustration indicates an area of life where you're doing something that doesn't work.
   c. Where are you frustrated in life?
2. Identify possible causes for your challenges and frustrations.
   a. What could you have been doing to cause these feelings?
   b. What things have you been doing that don't work for you?
   c. Create alternate actions you feel work in these situations.
   d. Be sure these actions from your new way of being.
   e. Write these moments down each time you notice them and the alternative actions you can take in the future.
3. Work to notice when you're in the midst of these situations and pause to substitute your alternate action.
4. Work to notice before you reach one of these situations and choose an alternate response for that situation as the moment

arises.

5. Evaluate the results you get by implementing these new actions.
    a. If you like the results rinse and repeat.
    b. If the results are unfavorable choose other actions.
    c. Test your new actions in the next challenging situation.
    d. Keep going until you get the desired results.
6. Begin to make the difference and choose to love your life.
7. Refer to Dale Carnegie's book, "How to Win Friends & Influence People," for more information on this subject and more.

WOULD YOU RATHER
BE RIGHT OR HAPPY?

~ A COURSE IN MIRACLES

~~~~~~~

EVERY SINGLE SECOND IS AN
OPPORTUNITY TO CHANGE YOUR LIFE,
BECAUSE IN ANY MOMENT YOU CAN
CHANGE THE WAY YOU FEEL.

~ RHONDA BYRNE

SMILES ARE FREE
PASS YOURS ON

~ CORY JENKINS

7

SHARE YOUR GIFTS

**Singing Karaoke with my family and friends during the holidays
Double D Karaoke- Brentwood, MO**

In college, I was technically forced to sing karaoke. Somewhere in my photos, I have a picture of me handcuffed to a karaoke DJ! Secretly, I wanted to sing but, at that time, I didn't have to courage to say so. I felt I needed it to seem as if I were being forced into it just in case I didn't do well. That was the first time I'd sung karaoke. It was also the first time I sang without someone or several people singing with me. I went from stage fright then, to singing with a band and then to singing in restaurants by myself. Now, whenever I see a band, I'm tempted to, and often do, ask if I can sit in. I created a bucket list for my trip to France and one item was to sing on the street. I accomplished this when I sat in with a street performer in Nice, France. Afterward, he asked me to come to the restaurant where he was performing later that night and sing with him. He was playing his guitar on the patio so we were technically still singing on the street. While singing with him, I noticed a couple of passers-by recording it. So... I went up to them after and asked if they would send me a copy. I wanted proof of checking that item off my bucket list since I'd now double accomplished my goal. I also sing karaoke every chance I get. I am perfectly happy singing alone these days.

There are still moments when I experience stage fright. For example when singing a song for the first time or singing in a more intimate setting for friends and loved ones. I'm better in crowds where it's less personal, but I can do both thanks to continually stretching myself beyond my comfort zone. The more you stretch the easier it gets until you end up with an expanded comfort zone. Like anything though, it takes practice.

Similar to my stage fright in my early days of singing, until recently, I would not allow myself to stand up as a voice of wisdom because I believed I wasn't worth listening to. I never gave myself permission to share my story with people other than friends and family. I felt my experience wouldn't make a difference because I still believed somewhere deep down that I was 'stupid'.

Later in life after taking several self-development courses, I wrote a talk that I felt would make a difference in people's lives. I planned on sharing and expanding that talk and turning it into a full weekend training or more. I gave the talk at several Kiwanis clubs and networking meetings, but I stopped short of setting up larger more impactful opportunities to speak. I did begin writing a book called "Love You to Health" and a teaser talk and course to go with it, but I stopped writing the book after moving to Utah. I shifted my focus to getting out of debt, began working in the hotel business and set everything else aside.

When I got singularly focused on my financial goals, I fell away from the normal healthy habits I had been practicing for so many years. I also set aside my dream to share the wisdom I had gathered over the years. I attained many financial goals during that period, but towards the end of my time in that industry, I realized that I had given up on my dream to make a real difference for people. I was able to reason with myself that I was making a difference for my clients, but knew I wanted more.

I still loved my life and several of my goals were being accomplished. These had been set long ago and were working on me subconsciously. I was accumulating rental properties as planned and paying off my debt. I was planning my future including the trip to Europe. However, I still wouldn't share or impart any of the wisdom or lessons that I had learned over the years because I didn't believe I was worthy of being heard. I also didn't feel I was worthy of love because I didn't really love myself. It was time to step out of my comfort zone again, step into love and take a leap of faith to share myself with people inside of my commitment to making a difference.

Therefore, I chose to quit my career with the hotels and give myself permission to really live my dreams and fall in love with myself. That's when everything started going in the right direction. I began to see more of the things I'd envisioned coming to pass in real life. Through the power of the law of attraction, things started working naturally for me.

Plans for Europe started falling into place. I started meeting people that fit into the puzzle of my life perfectly. It seemed they were purposefully placed in my path. Such as the opportunity allowing me to work while I was in Europe. People that had information I needed as well as people that needed information I had were also being placed into my life.

When you come from being somebody that loves yourself, what you get to provide for yourself and others is creating a life that you love. That love for yourself and your life creates your shine. This shine is what spreads to other people giving them permission to shine, as in the quote that starts this book by Marianne Williamson. By being your true self and loving you, you give other people permission to do the same.

It was during my trip to Europe that I realized that my mission was to share my love for life with other people. However, in order to share that love, I had to start loving myself and showing myself, love. This book is the culmination of that realization. Through loving myself I am now free to share my love for life with others.

I met Djana in Paris and we were both traveling to Nice and talked about getting together there. We had done some of the same coursework and she had already written a book. She was a powerful person but had lost her way. She'd been hurt and simply forgotten who she was. By the end of our time together in Nice, she thanked me and had taken action in her life that she'd been putting off for a while. She said that I was the turning point and had made a difference. She may not have known it yet, but she was the turning point for me as well. She made me realize that by sharing who I am and the love I have to give, I could make that difference I'd always wanted to make in the world.

I'd said I was going to write my book while away, but I had been making excuses not to. After our interaction, I was finally ready to start writing. However, I realized that my vision had grown and changed. The original book was to be called, 'Love You to Health,' but I now planned to write this book before and created the name, "I Love Myself So..." The intention behind the ellipses is to allow your mind to fill in the blank. How would you fill in the blank? You love yourself. So... what? What if you truly loved yourself? What would you be doing? What actions would you take? What actions would loving yourself give you? As was said in the earlier chapter, everything starts with being. So... if you come from 'who am I going to be in the matter of my life, in the matter of loving myself, in the matter of loving my friends and family,' what actions would that give you? So... there's the meaning behind the '...' and you get to fill in the missing words that fill that blank '...'

This book was born out of my quest to make a difference for people. It was made possible by my commitment to continue in the face of setbacks and challenges. I wasn't going to let my little health setback stop me from sharing my story or making a difference. I refused to let anything stop me any longer. I am the right person, it is the right time and I am committed to making a difference I was born to make.

So... instead of stopping, I chose to switch focus and write what I was ready to write. While I am working towards new health goals, I still love my life and fully believe everything happens for a reason. I was meant to write this book. I wouldn't have taken the time to write this book if I hadn't gotten fibroids to make me realize I needed to lower the stress in my life. This was what reminded me to respect and love my body. I was able to focus on the positives and remember that life is a journey and everything happens just right. I choose to enjoy every moment and celebrate my wins in life, like reducing my largest fibroid from 9 cm to 7 cm in just a few months with nutrition and stress reduction, I now get to live my book "Love You to Health" as I write it. I get the opportunity to live the transformation again and share health from a whole new level. I get to come from the standpoint of using my suggestions and living out the journey back to health through self-love.

My sharing is able to come from a place of love. I'm the same as everyone else but different at the same time. My version of making a difference might be just the thing certain people need to flip the switch and make a difference in their own life. My intention is that this then starts a chain reaction. The love they begin feeling for themselves, they now share with other people and begin a chain reaction that reaches further and further. This ripple will keep growing as long as we continue connecting with people and allowing our love and light to shine.

Your perfect imperfection may be just what someone needs to see to allow their perfectly imperfect light to shine and be just what someone else needs and so on. Several times since my encounter with Djana in Nice I've had people say that I said just the right thing to them at just the right time moment. Others have said I showed up at the perfect time in their life. Be it a first meeting or a call to a friend at just the right time. Once you open up to making a difference, the universe works to keep those ripples going. I've had several people show up for me in this way as well since I opened myself up to see and accept these little miracles. So... what miracles will you open yourself up to creating in your life and the lives of those around you. Will you use the moment after something happens to pause and think of the best response for your life?

Life lessons:

1. The more you do anything the easier it gets.
2. In order that share your gifts in a way that makes a difference, you must come from a loving place.
    a. People don't care how much you know until they know

how much you care.

    b. Seek first to understand before seeking to be understood.

    c. Refer again to Dale Carnegie's book, "How to Win Friends & Influence People," or Steven Covey's "The Seven Habits of Highly Effective People" for more information on this subject.

3. Buddha taught five things to consider before speaking. Is what you're saying:

    a. Factual and true

    b. Helpful or beneficial

    c. Spoken with kindness and good-will (that is, hoping for the best for all involved)

    d. Endearing (that is, spoken gently, in a way the other person can hear)

    e. Timely (occasionally something true, helpful, and kind will *not* be endearing, or easy for someone to hear, in which case we think carefully about *when* to say it)

Action steps:

1. List your gifts.

    a. What do you feel you were born to share with the world?

    b. What do you get compliments on?

    c. What do people thank you for?

2. In what ways do you already share your gifts?

3. List other ways you can share your gifts with the world.

4. How do your gifts make a difference for you and for others?

5. Practice pausing after someone stops speaking for a few reasons:

    a. They may not be finished.

    b. You then have time to consider your response.

        i. Be slow to criticize.

        ii. Start with a positive word.

        iii. Acknowledge what they've said first.

            1. It shows them respect.

            2. It allows them to feel heard.

            3. It also makes certain you understood.

            4. Your response can then be more easily accepted and heard.

c. When in doubt think:
   i. How do I want this conversation to turn out?
   ii. How will my words affect this relationship?
   iii. How can I make a positive impact?

LOVE ONLY GROWS BY SHARING.
YOU CAN ONLY HAVE MORE FOR YOURSELF
BY GIVING IT AWAY TO OTHERS.

~ BRIAN TRACY

~~~~~~~

WE MAKE A LIVING BY WHAT WE GET. WE
MAKE A LIFE BY WHAT WE GIVE.

~ WINSTON S. CHURCHILL

~~~~~~~

SOMETHING YOU SAY

MIGHT BE JUST THE THING THAT
SOMEONE YOU'RE WITH NEEDS TO HEAR.
SO... SHARE YOUR GIFT WITH LOVE.

~ CORY JENKINS

8

PERFECTLY IMPERFECT

Pulling faces on an ugly sweater run with friends
River Parkway- Ogden, Utah

Don't be afraid to be you and have fun with that. I used to never pull faces in pictures. I was afraid to look silly. Afraid to not be perfect! I always wanted to look presentable and appropriate. I didn't want to be embarrassed or look 'stupid.' Like I was ever perfect!?! Who is?! However, I am perfectly imperfect! So are you!

Here are a few sayings that I love. I've learned to be 'Positively Dissatisfied' or 'Positively Discontent.' You could also say 'Comfortably

Uncomfortable.' When you get comfortable with being uncomfortable you can accomplish great things! In other words, get used to being uncomfortable. Start staying in that space that stretches you into a new comfort zone. Be able to stretch and flow with life so that like a willow tree so you can bend and go with the flow of life; versus being like an oak tree, so rigid and stuck in your ways that you break in the storms of life. The key is to remember that there are two words in each phrase above. You must have both sides in order to grow and stretch yourself while remaining happy and content with your life and your accomplishments. It's all about balance. I've had some of the best experiences when I let go of the need to be perfect and pressure of having to do it right. It was uncomfortable but so worth it.

I love dancing as a couple but I have always had to force myself to dance alone. I quit being a cheerleader in high school and shied away from my thought of dancing with the Sugar Bear dancers in college for this reason. I was afraid of being the center of attention. It's still something I overcome each time I am faced with the opportunity. We all have our weaknesses.

One night on a trip to visit my friends in Belgium, we went to a late-night dance club. When we got out on the dance floor I decided to let loose and let go of my inhibitions. My reward this particular evening was one of the nicest, most sincere compliments I've received in a long time. I get compliments on my smile or eyes which were inherited. I get complimented on my voice which is something I've worked at, but again the base of which was handed to me by my parents. I even get compliments when I go out partner dancing, but that is still dependant on someone else. However, that night, while I was dancing alone on the dance floor, a twenty-something-year-old girl came over and told me that she loved the way I danced. It was quite hilarious when she had to explain it again to my friend who actually spoke her language, but she was sweet enough to do it anyway.

I remember thinking as I went out on the floor that I was older than most people in the bar, including my friend Max who I was visiting. My clothes were somewhat different than most people in the bar that night as I wasn't from there and wasn't knowledgeable about local fashions. I remember letting go of all of that in favor of having fun and it worked. I danced more than any of my friends that night and had a great time doing so. I also caused a huge smile to form on the face of the girl giving me the compliment. The real key to loving your life is noticing the small miracles, loving and being grateful for all the beautiful little details. Love and accept all the beauty that is you! If you were anyone else, or in any way different from who you truly are, then you wouldn't make the difference you were born to make. Let your light shine! Everything in life is a choice. You get to choose to love life and live it powerfully! So... What will you choose to do with the '...' at the end of the statement, I Love Myself So...? So... What?

Life Lessons:

1. Accept your perfect imperfection and that of others.
2. Let go of judgment, fear and worrying what others think and you'll let go of stress and enjoy life!
3. Give compliments freely and often. You never know how much it will mean to the person receiving them.
4. What other people think of you is none of your business unless it benefits you. Constructive criticism is a great tool when requested. However, check in with your intuition to be sure that their suggestions are a fit for the direction you are choosing for your life before acting upon anyone's opions or advice. Create your own opinions and run with them.
    a. Pay attention to common sense and decency. As long as your version of fun is only affecting you and others in a positive way, you're fine.
    b. When your fun affects someone else, then their opinion does matter. Be respectful, courteous and treat others as you feel they'd want to be treated.
5. "Treat others as *you* would want to be treated" is the Golden Rule. In the lesson above, I'm referring to the Platinum Rule. "Treat others as *they* want to be treated."
6. Pay attention and ask questions and get to know the people in your life. This will help you in so many areas.
7. Everything is better when you're doing something you love.

8. Surround yourself with great people and your life will continue to improve!
9. Life is a choice! You can choose to love it and live it powerfully!
10. Let your perfectly imperfect light shine and brighten the world, freeing other so do the same as well!

Action Steps:

1. Check out these sources for more information on the above lessons. Look into learning more about the people that you love and work with. Discover their Love Languages, Color Codes, Meyers Briggs or DISC types. These sources can assist you in relating to and using 'The Platinum Rule' to treat them the way they want to be treated.
   a. How to Win Friends and Influence People - Dale Carnegie
   b. Don't Sweat the Small Stuff - Richard Carlson
   c. The Four Agreements - Don Miguel Ruiz
   d. The 5 Languages of Love - Gary Chapman
   e. The Myers Briggs test - mbtionline.com
   f. The DISC test - discpersonalitytesting.com
   g. The Color Code- Taylor Hartman
      i. Taylor Hartman books
      ii. The Color Code Online Personality Test
   h. The Platinum Rule - Dr. Tony Alessandra-
      i. www.alessandra.com/abouttony/aboutpr.asp
      ii. www.youtube.com/tonyalessandra
      iii. youtu.be/rRB-504Wn3M
2. Write down several options to fill in the blank after this statement.
   a. I Love Myself So...
   b. So... What?
   c. Create something to fill in the '...' for yourself.
   d. Use this question or these answers to inspire you the next time you have a choice to make.

Imperfection is beauty, madness is genius and it's better to be absolutely ridiculous than absolutely boring.

~ Marilyn Monroe

YOU'VE GOTTA DANCE
LIKE THERE'S NOBODY WATCHING,
LOVE LIKE YOU'LL NEVER BE HURT,
SING LIKE THERE'S NOBODY LISTENING,
AND LIVE LIKE IT'S HEAVEN ON EARTH.

~ WILLIAM PURKEY

SECTION TWO

The Life Story That Will Lead

You to Create a Life You Love

THOUGH NO ONE CAN GO
BACK AND
MAKE A BRAND NEW
START,
ANYONE CAN START
FROM NOW AND
MAKE A BRAND NEW
ENDING.

~ CARL BARD

9

REINVENTING YOU

Already cleaning cars at Grandma's house
Cedar Hill, Missouri

From a young age, I learned the value of hard work. In the picture above I was about to turn two years old. At that age, I lived with my grandmother and my Aunt Betty weekdays. Mom worked full time, went to school at night and had me on weekends. She had my brother full-time because he was already in school. This kept her from having to pay for daycare for me. My grandmother and aunt took a lot of the weight off of her shoulders this way.

When it was time for preschool, I started staying with my mom full-time in Clayton, Missouri. I went to a little preschool just down the street from our apartment. I made a few friends and we got to stay together as we moved over to grade school. My mom bought a condo right across the street from the school which meant I could simply walk across the street for the first two years.

Since I was born in December, my mom had a choice. She could either allow me to start kindergarten a little late or have me skip kindergarten altogether. This would mean starting first grade early. She chose to have me take the necessary tests and skip kindergarten. Going straight into first grade was just fine because Mrs. Baker, the first-grade teacher, was amazing. However, I was still in a different class than the few friends I'd made in preschool.

When I got to second grade my teacher called me out for asking so many questions. She said, "Class, the reason Cory is so stupid and asks so many questions, is that she skipped kindergarten so she's younger than everyone here." You don't realize how words like that affect you until years later. Now to be fair, that is how my five-year-old self remembers it. It's possible that she didn't actually use the word 'stupid', but that was what I was left with.

I spent well over twenty years of my life trying to prove I wasn't 'stupid'. Not trying to prove that I was actually smart, but trying to prove that I wasn't 'stupid'. Some would argue that this actually benefited me by causing me to become a near straight-A student. Others might berate the teacher for being so careless with her words. Both could be considered true. It all depends on perspective. I now choose the more empowering context that she pushed me to excel with her words.

Several things happened from that point on through high school which had me withdraw further and further from socializing. One of the most damaging took place with my friend's older brother. I had to have been about five and her brother was about eighteen. When I went over to my friend's house to play, he was there and wanted to play with us. Unfortunately, he wanted to play doctor and given my age I didn't know that was inappropriate. Let's just say his specialty was going to be gynecology. At least he kept it 'professional' so that nothing but his finger defiled me. Let's also say that I never went over to her house again.

That experience left me questioning what behavior was appropriate. It also, once I realized what had happened wasn't appropriate, left me feeling like I wasn't clean anymore. I began to feel that I needed to make up for that somehow.

I spent years trying to make up for that, as well as other things that happened around that age. This attempt at atonement continued all the way up to and through my marriage. I dated several people before I got married and had a lot of fun; some in high school, many more in college and beyond. However, I always felt like I should 'save myself' for marriage. This was due in part to my being raised Christian by my dad and partly due to these childhood experiences. I felt this need to redeem myself, in order to be worthy of the man I'd marry.

Ultimately, I did everything, aside from sex for reproduction, before marriage. I saved that for my husband. Many of my misgivings about being with men came from these earthy childhood experiences. I'm sure that several of my relationships ended due to the shame I still felt and the fact that I wouldn't share what happened. It took years and several self-development courses before I could share this with anyone.

I went through grade school feeling like I didn't fit in. When I got to middle school I thought maybe I could start fresh. I decided to start using my middle name to pretend I was a different person. I had my teachers calling me Liz, short for Elizabeth. I soon realized that many of the kids came from my grade school and already knew me, so it didn't work. Finally, my math teacher said, "Liz, I never get a response when I call you by your name. Are you sure I can't call you Cory?" That's when I switched back to using my first name.

Recently, as I was going thru items to move, I found a gym shirt from middle school that said Liz on the back. My first thought was actually, *How did I end up with Liz's shirt?* It probably took me a full minute to realize that it was actually my shirt! Needless to say, my first experience with reinventing myself was unsuccessful. It seems I needed a few more life lessons before I could successfully reinvent myself.

Later in school, one of my classmates came up to me and asked if I had had sex with my brother. In astonishment, I quickly replied, "No!" However, I now knew that rumors had been spreading. Not only had they spread about what had happened with my friend's brother, but also with my brother's friends. They did random things to me like pants me to wake me up. This realization had me withdraw even further. I started spending evenings at home watching TV or working on homework versus going out and having fun. I didn't gain too much weight at that point, but enough that it was uncomfortable. Around the age of fifteen, I decided to change that and hit the gym.

Until the last half of high school, I was quite shy. With the introduction of a new best friend and the gym, I broke out of my shyness a bit. However, one of the other things introduced around that time was alcohol. One of my first few experiences with alcohol shaped my use of it to this day. It was the first and only time I did not remember much of what had happened the night before. Luckily, my friends and my brother were there to take care of me. I had no idea that I had consumed too much since I didn't have any real experience with alcohol at the time; thus, why you shouldn't be drinking at the ripe young age of fifteen.

We'd gone to an underage dance bar that we went to every weekend. However, this time, before going in, we downed about half a fifth of vodka mixed with fruit punch. That was a 'bit' excessive between just two teenage girls. Unfortunately, I think I got the lion's share. I was already feeling the effects when we walked in. I remember dancing a little, hitting on a guy that was not at all interested and throwing up in the bathroom. That's it. When I came out of the stall, I recall looking down, picking up my hair and asking, "Why is my hair red?" I had no idea I'd just thrown up all over my hair. My friend had to explain that, which is why I remembered that fact.

When I got home my brother got me a bagel, some Tylenol and a big glass of water to help avoid a hangover. It worked pretty well. I woke up with cotton mouth and remember thinking the night had been a bad dream. I quickly realized it wasn't when I tried getting out of bed and was so dizzy I had to sit back down.

I noticed I had bruises on my knees and when I asked my friend what happened she said I fell on the way to the bathroom. I thought, '*What a relief! That meant it was in a small corridor and no-one saw me.*' It wasn't until about ten years later, after college, when we became roommates for a year, that she finally told me the whole truth. I had fallen right in the middle of the club. Those were the days of flare shirts and skirts and I had on both that night. I know I looked like a complete idiot in front of everyone. That may be why she told me way later. She may have wanted to be able to go back to the club. She had to know that I wouldn't want to if I had known I made such a fool of myself. She may also have thought it would be kind to save me from the embarrassment of knowing the truth.

I realized later that drinking to fit in had affected my learning that year in school. I went from a straight-A student to getting a C in one class. I audited another class because I knew I wasn't going to get a good grade. Luckily, I still graduated high school with a great overall GPA. This was most likely due to the fact that I cut back on drinking after that experience. Other than a wine cooler at New Year's and one off-campus party with a girlfriend in college, I didn't drink again after highschool until I turned twenty-one.

I even chose the college that I thought would be less of a party school. In my day, the University of Missouri, Columbia (MIZZOU) was Missouri's party school. Southwest Missouri State University (SMSU- Now called MSU- Missouri State University, Springfield) was not seen as a party school. Therefore, I thought I could get a better education there with less distraction. Oddly enough, by the end of my college days, it was the party school of Missouri. However, I didn't realize that until after I'd graduated magna cum laude. Thank goodness I chose to learn from my mistakes.

I still attended all the frat parties I wanted to and had an amazing time. I met awesome people and made great friends. However, it never needed to include alcohol. It was actually more fun having people try to get me to drink than it was actually drinking. I loved to watch people make drunken fools of themselves. It was hilarious. Even after turning twenty-one I still seldom drank. Notice I said after turning twenty-one. This is because I would call the amount of drinking I did at my two twenty-first birthday parties a 'little' excessive. My best friend from college threw a surprise party for me in Springfield. It was so fun. I had a few long island iced teas with my friends and danced a ton that night. Then she came to Saint Louis to celebrate with me, my brother and my best friend from high school. I had my crew around me to make sure no poor decision making took place and we had a sober driver too. Planning is key to letting loose in a fun, safe environment.

I had a wonderful college experience even though I barely drank and stayed a virgin. In fact, people who didn't know me may have thought I was a drunken slut because I went to so many parties. Others may have thought me a prude. I didn't care. I had a blast and people, who took the time to get to know me and truly mattered to me, had a blast with me!

As a resident assistant, I went to Panama City with the girls from my floor a few times. I dated a few frat boys, cheerleaders, and wrestlers. A few of those relationships ended because I wanted to stay a virgin. However, none of us were ready for a serious commitment, so it was for the best. I made an impression though. Later, I saw one of the frat boys I had dated at a bar where I loved to go dancing. He introduced me to his fiancée. When she stepped away, he whispered in my ear that she was a virgin. I guess I'd set a precedence.

I chose to go college a few hours away from Saint Louis so that I could have the experience of starting fresh. In high school, I was always scared to be myself. I wanted the opportunity to step outside that comfort zone and experience being 'me' for the first time without the fear of what people would think of me. I always held back in high school because I was afraid of people judging me, making fun of me, or laughing at me, etcetera. I wanted to start fresh in college and reinvent myself and I did.

I didn't realize it at the time, but that was one of my first experiences with successfully reinventing myself. I chose to be someone in charge of, and in control of, my own life. In college, I felt free to create a 'me' that reflected who I truly was. I was open, fun, engaging and unabashedly outgoing. I also shed the freshman 15 pounds instead of gaining them. A person would wonder how I stayed up all night having fun with my friends, got straight A's and was a resident assistant all at the same time. I definitely burnt the candle at both ends and had a blast doing it.

Sometimes it takes a good lesson to wake a person up. Since then, I've never been a huge drinker. If I know I have good friends around that I trust will watch out for me, then I'm comfortable letting loose and having a few. Even just having a few can inhibit my decision-making ability. I've learned that having your wits about you can keep you from embarrassing yourself like I did and/or out of harm's way. So... I've never forgotten an evening after that night. I enjoy drinking, but it's never been a big part of my life. So I'm thankful that I chose to learn from that experience at an early age, versus repeating it. I know many children these days aren't choosing the path that will lead them to a rewarding life and I'm saddened by that fact. Neither drugs nor alcohol are answers to any challenge. Facing challenges head-on, with a clear mind, is the only path I've ever found to bring satisfaction.

You can reinvent yourself at any moment. You're never stuck with the way you are unless you can't see the way you truly want to be. As Walt Disney said, "If you can dream it, you can do it!" Start dreaming! The beautiful thing about dreams and reinventing yourself is that you never have to keep a dream you create or the 'you' you've invented. Try them on like a coat in the store of life and if you don't like it, let it go. Hang it back up on the rack and leave it there. You may want to revisit that rack later, but you aren't stuck with it! You have the freedom to create something new!

That's one of the things they say about all the tools you're given in courses like Landmark Education. Try the tools on like a coat and if you don't like them, leave them there. Landmark Education assisted me in reinventing myself after I got out of college and took a job that didn't serve me.

Right out of college I moved in with my best friend from high school and took a job as an overnight supervisor. Because I majored in International Business and minored in French, I'd found a position in a reservation

CORY JENKINS

agency for international travelers. I managed the people they hired who spoke foreign languages and set up reservations for cell phones. Yes, people used to rent cell phones when they traveled for business. Unfortunately, I let this overnight schedule throw my health out of whack and gained about 40 pounds. I knew this wasn't where I was committed to being, so I reinvented myself.

Just because you feel you've 'arrived' at any given point in life doesn't mean you 'have' to stay there. If you 'arrive' and then realize it's not what you thought, or that it doesn't fit or work for your life, you can choose to reinvent yourself!

NOTE: It also doesn't mean you will get stay there. 'Arriving' doesn't guarantee you a permanent spot. You will need to continually work on your dreams or your health or whatever it is you're going for if it's something you want to keep.

I got a different job, joined a gym with my boyfriend and began shedding the weight. It was about this time that my mom introduced me to Landmark Education and I began taking courses to transform my life. With that new job, I paid off the few thousand I had on credit cards and my car and I was looking to buy a house at the ripe old age of about twenty-four.

However, it was at this point, that my mom asked me a very important question. She said 'Are you sure you want to buy a house right now? You could travel for a while and figure out where you really want to live and then buy a house there.' I realized she was right. I really hadn't traveled very much around the US at that point. I also wasn't sure Saint Louis was where I wanted to buy my first house and settle down. So... I planned to set off, I thought just around the country, to visit friends, experience new cities and figure out which one felt like home to me. The time off and this trip turned out to be so much more.

Life Lessons:

1. You can reinvent yourself at any point!
2. You're never stuck with anything you create.
3. Don't let anyone hold you back from being who you truly want to be.
4. You can always create something that inspires and empowers you!

Action Steps:

1. Who are you? Take some time to write down how you see yourself right now. By this, I mean all of the amazing qualities you already possess.
2. Who do you long to be? Take some time to write down all of the qualities you'd like to cultivate in yourself.
3. Who in your life has these qualities that you admire?
4. What results or things do they have that you long for?
5. What your life would look like if you were this person you long to be?
    a. Write down a description of a day in your perfect life.
    b. Describe yourself as the person you long to be in the present tense. Example: I am free, fun, engaging and charismatic.
    c. What would you be doing?
    d. List some results that are important to you?

LIFE ISN'T ABOUT FINDING YOURSELF.
LIFE IS ABOUT CREATING YOURSELF.

~ GEORGE BERNARD SHAW

NOTHING IS,
UNLESS OUR THINKING MAKES IT SO.

~ SHAKESPEARE

10

SEIZE OPPORTUNITIES
Grandpa ~ Tell Me 'Bout the Good Ole Days

Watching Grandpa throw a perfect net on a visit at ten years old
Cut Off, Louisiana

When I first chose to take time off work to travel and figure out where I wanted to live, my grandfather fell ill. At that time, my mom worked full time, my brother lived in the San Francisco area and my aunt had just had back surgery. I was thought of as the baby of the family, so no one thought of me to take on being his caregiver. Needless to say, my mother was astonished when I offered to drive down to Louisiana and take care of him.

I was, of course, the obvious choice given my new found freedom. So... I made plans to go live with Grandpa. This way I could take him to his doctor's appointments and learn the details of his health challenges. Little did I know that it would prove to be the most amazing opportunity to get to know my grandfather that I would ever have!

In a few weeks, we'd finished the doctor's appointments and explanations. Through all of it, I got to listen to stories about his life and spend the time with him that I'd never had. The most personal moment I had with my grandfather and ironically the time I felt the closest to him was when he trusted me to clip his toenails. Gross, I know, but it turned into a very endearing moment. He had been living in Louisiana for a long time while most the family lived in Missouri.

We set an appointment to get him a pacemaker that fell on the week of Thanksgiving. I asked if it would be safe to take him to Saint Louis to be with family for the holiday. The doctor assured us several times that this would be fine. The trick was getting my grandpa to believe the doctor.

Thanksgiving was only two days after his surgery. The thought of driving for thirteen hours in a car with his granddaughter from Baton Rouge, Louisiana to Saint Louis, Missouri must have been terrifying. Not to mention the fact that he'd be spending almost a week away from his home. That was probably a bit stressful all by itself.

We talked it over, and over, and over. Finally, I let him convince me that it would be better if I were to go alone. He said he would prefer to stay behind. After all, he had lived alone for years and rarely came to Thanksgiving as it was. So... we got his medications and everything else set up for him to manage while I was away. Then the next day, just as I finished getting ready to leave for Saint Louis, he said, 'Cory, I think I will go with you after all.' It was literally a miracle.

I had fully expected him to go, but at the same time chose to give him the space to choose his own response. Instead of working hard to convince him of my way of thinking I acknowledged that I understood his uncertainty about traveling after his pacemaker surgery. I also shared that I really wanted him there with me for Thanksgiving and that the family said they would love to see him too. In taking the time to acknowledge his concerns and by sharing my desires from the heart, I created an opening for him to make an informed choice. He was able to hear what I shared because I first acknowledged that I understood his point of view. In doing so I created an opening for him to say yes!

We then spent the next two hours getting him ready to go. This meant that we weren't able to leave until approximately one in the afternoon. Given that it was about a thirteen-hour car ride, we were now looking at arriving in St. Louis at about two in the morning. It was going to be a long day. However, it would turn out to be an amazing experience for the whole family.

The car ride was our first adventure. I got to learn some fun things not only about my grandpa, but also about my grandma. This included the fact that I sometimes spoke to my grandpa just like grandma used to. We were driving along and we both thought it sounded like we had a flat tire. The first two times, at my grandfather's request, I got out and checked it, but there was nothing wrong. I decided it must be that hitting all of the lines in the road was just creating the flat tire sound. The third time it started my grandfather asked me to stop the car to check the tires again. However, this time I was pretty sure that it was the road, so after some debate, he finally said, "alright Clara." This, by the way, was my grandmother's name. He said, "Your grandma was just a stubborn as you are." I politely won the battle on stopping and had a cute moment with my grandpa in the process.

When we got to Saint Louis we are greeted by my mother. For Thanksgiving that year we had a house full of guests. My favorite part of that Thanksgiving was that my family went with me to a karaoke bar and I got to sing a song for each of them. I had learned 'Sunday Kind of Love' in the style of Reba McEntire for my aunts, 'Crazy' by Patsy Cline for my mom, a song by No Doubt for my brother and 'Grandpa' by the Judds for my grandpa. I got to dance with my grandfather while singing one of my songs and it was a moment I will cherish forever.

That Thanksgiving was one of the best. It was wonderful to have the whole family together. It was the last time my grandfather would make it up to Saint Louis. He passed away the following year. My choice to take that year off created a moment in time with my grandfather that I will always hold dear. That experience would never have been possible if I'd not taken a leap of faith to follow my gut and reach for my dreams. I continued on to fulfill the dream of traveling around the country visiting friends and looking for my next place to call home. However, I'm so thankful that I paused to seize that opportunity. I would never have had another chance to capture that experience. You never know when it might be your last moment with someone you care about or even with someone you just met.

Life Lessons:

1. Expect miracles.
2. Seize Opportunities.
3. Look for ways to create miracles.
4. Look for ways to connect with people.
5. Seek first to understand, then to be understood.
6. Look for ways to bring joy to others. In doing so you'll naturally create joy in your own life.
7. Cherish time with loved ones because you never know how long you'll have them in your life.

Action Steps: Answer these questions in your journal:

1. Where in your life do you see opportunities to connect with people?
2. Where are you taking advantage of those opportunities?
3. What more can you do about that? Where can you connect?

4. Where might you be missing out on opportunities and experiences to connect in your life?
5. How would seizing opportunities impact your life for the better?
6. Refer to <u>Steven Covey's "7 Habits of Highly Effective People"</u> for more information on seeking first to understand, then to be understood.
7. Refer to <u>"The Secret" by Rhonda Byrne</u> to learn about expecting, attracting and creating miracles.

GRANDPA,
TELL ME ABOUT THE GOOD OLD DAYS.
SOMETIMES IT SEEMS LIKE,
THIS WORLD'S GONE CRAZY.

~ THE JUDDS

11

GETTING OUT OF THE COMFORT ZONE
A Year of Exploration

Twenty-five - Having fun while visiting my friend at her studio (met working at Sears Portrait Studio's headquarters in St. Louis) Sears Portrait Studio- Goldsboro, North Carolina

After my time at Grandpa's, I began my adventures. To kick it off, I took a trip by myself to Las Vegas. I spent my birthday at a dance competition there. It was one of my first trips alone where I wouldn't be visiting friends or family. It was quite liberating. I danced the weekend away with new friends and sang live at one of the evening events just for fun. Coincidentally, this was my first time singing without a karaoke screen in front of me or my dad or choir beside me. I believe this trip created my travel bug and gave me the knowledge that I could go out traveling on my own and have a blast.

I also visited friends from my summer studying at Laval University in Quebec. I spent three weeks in Montreal, where they'd moved. It was an amazing visit with my friend Melanie and her Brother Guillaume. I've been trying to reconnect with her ever since and cannot find her. If you happen to read this and know the LaPlants, please let me know! Those were the days before cell phones, the internet, and Facebook.

While working at CPI Photo Finishing/Sears Portrait Studios I met several managers over the phone. However, I only connected with and kept in touch with one of them. I visited her and her family in North Carolina. This is where the photo above was taken. We were in her studio having fun during my visit. I'd never done a session in one of our studios while working there. Back then everything was printed, thus the lines through the photo.

I stayed and traveled with her several times throughout my year of exploration. We even went to D.C. with her whole family. We put together a plan to connect with a guy I met in college on my last spring break. He drove up from his place in Virginia to meet us in D.C. We then left the kids with her parents in Pennsylvania and continued to New York for the weekend. We had some amazing times.

Later that year, she set me up on a couple of blind dates while I was in North Carolina. I dated and visited one of them in Ohio and then he set me up to stay with his friend in LA when I visited California. It was a footloose and fancy-free time in my life. The year off work provided me so many amazing opportunities and adventures. It was priceless!

In searching out my next career, I looked into working with a network marketing company in the travel industry. They marketed educational retreats in exciting destinations around the world. I went on retreats in Egypt, Cancun, and cities around the US. This adventurous business had its pluses and minuses. The upsides were the travel and learning opportunities. I took a tax seminar that taught me about writing off business and travel expenses as well as other inspirational self-development seminars. The downside was the cost of these courses and their business structure. Their plan had you selling for the person above you at first and not earning quickly enough for my taste.

When I finished my year of traveling I had racked up over $30,000 in debt. The good news was that I became extremely creative in financing and managing debt and credit cards. I was able to transfer debt and never pay full interest rates. On average I only paid 3% interest on the debt. Thanks to this it took me only two years of concentrated effort to eliminate this debt.

There are many intricacies involved in getting and keeping your credit score up and your debt in check. However, that's the main thing that's saved me whenever I've chosen to go into debt. I've always buckled down and paid things off. That meant living below my means. In other words, it means I spent less than I earned and put everything extra either into saving for a trip or paying off the last trip. The key that allowed me to love my life, even while living on a budget, was that I knew that I was saving for or paying for my dreams.

I have no regrets. I realized I am, have been and always will be willing to pay a little interest to have an experience that lasts a lifetime. I know I will always have a realistic plan in place to pay things off, So... I make sure everything works out. Many people believe in living with no debt. It is definitely more practical to save for your goals and dreams. I started doing this later in life.

Your dreams may be different than mine. They may include a great education for your kids or a beautiful home in an area you love or even a new car. Planning for these is essential. Going into debt without a clear plan for getting out is like running into a burning building and not knowing the escape route. I'm not promoting going into debt. I am promoting living a life you love. If that involves going into debt for a short moment to create a lasting memory, for me, I say so be it.

Disclaimer: In order for the aforementioned plan to work, you must already have good credit. You must have the ability to access extremely low-interest rates. I don't want to lead you down a path to insurmountable debt.

Some of the courses I've taken have taught me how to raise credit scores after financial setbacks. I learned about negotiating with creditors to lower interest rates to pay off debt quickly. I also learned how to stack and manage payments to repair credit. I used all of this information to save thousands in interest and maintain a good credit score.

If you have an interest in this area, there are several sources that can assist you. However, PLEASE don't do a 'debt consolidation'. Many times those are scams that will actually hurt your credit and cost you thousands. Much of what they do can be done by you on the phone in a few hours. This information, if needed, can greatly assist you in living a life you love. So... don't wait till I write a book about that. This book is about loving your life not managing your credit score. If you would like to set up coaching with me about managing your debt or credit score, feel free to contact me for information. My email is: Cory@ILoveMyselfSo.com

Now back to your regularly scheduled program.

On one adventure with the travel company, I chose to save a little money. I took a Greyhound bus to get to New York for my flight to Egypt, but we arrived in Ohio, in the middle of the night, to find the drivers had gone on strike. You may run into challenges with frugal travel or any travel for that matter. The trick is in how you handle those challenges. It looked like I was stuck indefinitely. My flight out of JFK left the next day and the way it was looking, Greyhound was not going to get me there.

At this point, my 'can do' attitude went into overdrive. I started talking to everyone in line. I found two other people in the same predicament. We all had flights out of New York the next day. After a bit of discussion, I used my powers of persuasion to convince them to split the cost of renting a car and drive the rest of the way to New York. If we joined together, we could all still make our flights.

It's this kind of 'can-do' attitude that will get you ahead in life! Due to our quick thinking and teamwork, we all made our flights and I was able to experience Egypt.

Upon arrival, I met my group at our resort, the Mena House Oberoi. We were greeted with jasmine leis as we entered the poolside patio for our welcome party. The next day we went by limo to a perfumery where I found jasmine perfume that matched the gorgeous scent of those flowers. Now I could remember this trip and that scent forever.

I also had the honor of being asked to sing in the lobby of the resort. I was sitting with my friends when they started playing a song I knew and I couldn't help but sing along. After a minute or two, the piano player asked if I would come up next to him at the piano and sing for everyone. For a moment I hesitated, but it was just too amazing an opportunity to pass up. After that, every night as I passed by the lobby, the piano player would stop me and ask me to sing Celine Dion's "My Heart Will Go On". It was quite a compliment and it was so much fun getting to sing aside a grand piano in the lobby of an amazingly beautiful resort.

Another such experience was being given a gorgeous robe in the style worn to a Bedouin party in the desert. We were taken on camelback to tents set up with a tantalizing spread of food, drinks, and entertainment. It was quite interesting learning how to control a camel. I wanted to take pictures of my friends so I end up turning around and riding backward on my camel for part of the ride. It was awesome. However, my last and most awe-inspiring experience was by far superior.

In a tomb, at the top of one of the pyramids in Giza, I started singing amazing grace. I wanted to hear how my voice would echo and reverberate off the walls. I didn't expect that another girl who happened to be there would join me in singing. Our voices fit well together and the beautiful harmony reverberated off the walls and echoed down the stairs for everyone to enjoy. It was an absolutely beautiful moment.

Life Lessons:

1. Listen to your gut.
2. Look for opportunities to enjoy new experiences.
3. Get out of your comfort zone.
4. Plan for your dreams.
5. Spend less than you earn.

6. Save for expenses or create an escape route for any debt incurred.
7. Do what's necessary to maintain or improve your credit score.

Action Steps:
Work on these questions in your journal:

1. What places or things have you always wanted to visit or experience?
2. What memories have you always wanted to make?
3. Where are you holding yourself back in life?
4. What would you do if you had an unlimited supply of money?
5. What would you do if you had time freedom?
6. What would it take for you to make those things happen for you given your current circumstances?
7. What negative mindset or beliefs would you need to let go of to allow your dreams to become reality?
8. What empowering belief will you create now to shift your focus to believing in yourself and your ability to create what you want in life?
9. What actions will you take to keep that belief in the forefront of your thoughts?
   a. Will you read it aloud each day?
   b. Will you write it out each day?
   c. Will you put it on a mirror so you see it each morning?
   d. Will you write it on a notecard to keep with you all day?
   e. Will you do all of the above?
10. What structures will you need in place to assist you in creating this new reality for yourself?
    a. Will you tell a few friends or family members so they can hold you accountable?
    b. Will you write out all the action steps and milestones?
    c. Will you find a partner to go the distance with you?

IF YOU ARE ALWAYS TRYING TO BE NORMAL,
YOU WILL NEVER KNOW HOW
AMAZING
YOU CAN BE.

~ MAYA ANGELOU

LIFE BEGINS AT THE END OF YOUR
COMFORT ZONE.

~ NEALE DONALD WALSCH

12

ALWAYS BE CREATING
Two Tickets to Paris

**The 'Red Dress' worn atop the Eiffel Tower in Paris, France
Pictured here a few years later at a conference
Salt Lake City, Utah**

Once through with my year of exploration I came back home and decided to work for my best friend. My plan was to stay with my mom for a bit while paying off my debt. I also planned to build-up my Juice Plus business enough to allow me to work solely for myself and move to another city.

At this point, I was taking leadership courses with Landmark Education and chose to sign up to take a few of them in San Francisco. My brother lived in the South Bay Area. So... I figured this trip would be a great opportunity to visit him and see more of San Francisco. The last time I visited him, we didn't spend too much time in the city.

During the leadership course, they announced a job opening for the executive assistant (EA) to the CEO of Landmark Education. This person would be working at their world headquarters in San Francisco. I chose to take a leap of faith and apply for the position. I started interviewing the following week.

In the second course, I met John, who offered me a place to stay in the city. This would make it easier to get to my interviews at Landmark. The first time I visited the area I stayed with my brother, south of the city. We only drove up once to see the tourist attractions. This was my first time seeing San Francisco through a local's eyes and I fell in love. Now I was truly excited about the possibility of moving there.

The last course was called the communication course. Everyone referred to it as the love course, but I had chosen to work on my finances. As I mentioned, the travel during my year of exploring had left me in a 'bit' of debt. Therefore, I felt I needed to focus on getting out of debt and back on my feet financially. However, after chatting with a few participants over lunch, they shared a different idea with me. They said that I might want to work on my relationships with men. They thought I had a commitment issue. I tried to convince them I had a 'finding the right guy' issue. In the end, however, I chose to take them up on their challenge.

I started by creating a way of 'being' because as I said before, it all starts with 'being'. That went fine. I created 'being' *free, open, playful and passionate in all of my relationships.* However, I was completely baffled when asked to create a goal that I would achieve a year from that day. I mean, how do you create a relationship out of nothing?!?! I had no idea where to start.

This is where I got brave. I was dating a few guys at home but no one seemed like the 'one.' To say in front of a group that I needed help on my finances was one thing, but to share that I wanted help finding the right guy was something completely different. I could've sat back and worked on my project from my seat. Though I don't believe I would've have gotten half as much from the course from my seat. So... I stepped out of my comfort zone to share a part of my life that some would see as private or embarrassing. I felt exposed and raw but I did it!

I raised my hand to get coaching on my relationships. Standing there, in front of everyone, I was asked to describe what I would accomplish in the next year out of being the free, open, playful, and passionate person I was now committed to being. I said, "I'll have a committed relationship." The course leader's reply was, "That sounds like a death sentence coming out of your mouth."

I was asked to describe what a fly on the wall would see if they looked at my life in a year. What would I physically have to show for 'being' free, open, playful and passionate? What could someone see that would show them that I had reached my goal or attained the objective?

I remember thinking *I have no idea what to say. What in the world could I create to have a year from now to show that I had been free open, playful, and passionate in all of my relationships? How could somebody see that I had been all of those things?* I paused and stepped into my new way of 'being' and then asked myself what would it look like if I had an amazing relationship? I cleared my mind and out of nowhere, I said, "I'll have two tickets to Paris, reservations at the top of the Eiffel Tower, a red dress, flowers and I'll be with a man who loves me that I love. She said, "Now that I can see." I remember, at that moment, thinking *ok, but I can't see it.* When asked to create a plan to get there in a year, I thought *Really?!?*

How do you plan to get into an amazing relationship and end up in Paris? I had to break it down into 'doable' steps that I could see and knew I could accomplish. I now knew who I was going to be, but what actions could I take from there. Breaking it down into a six-month milestone, one-month plan, and a one-week goal helped. I remember saying that in one month I'd go on six dates and buy the red dress. I wrote that I would have the red dress in a week and would have gone on two dates.

Now you have to remember that I was in San Francisco and not my hometown Saint Louis. I'd arrived just over one week prior to saying I'd go on two dates within a week! However, I knew I'd met a guy at the airport and someone in the leadership course so I knew I could commit to going on two dates. That week I went out on a date every night for the four nights leading up to the last night of the course. I went out with two people from the leadership course, the man I'd met at the airport on my way into town and someone I'd met out shoe shopping.

The last night of the course, John went with me to buy the red dress and we stopped for dinner before heading over to the course. During the evening I ended up sitting next to one of the men we'd had lunch with earlier that week when it was recommended that I work on my relationships. I'd since taken notice of him a few times throughout the course. At the end of the night, as we were saying our goodbyes, he and I set a date for the next day.

John and I then went back to his apartment on Russian Hill. His window looked out over the city, but he said that the best view was the view from the top of the hill. So... we decided to grab a glass of wine and some of the baklava I'd made the night before and walked up the hill. Once outside, I felt a chill and John immediately put his suit coat around my shoulders as we took off for the top of the hill. Once there, taking in the view, I looked at him and realized this was a seriously romantic moment. I also realized that I was with an extremely attractive man who was fun, witty, charming and handsome. I thought to myself *why am I not dating this man?* So... I turned to him and said, "You know, I really value our friendship, but you're also really attractive and I'm curious as to how you kiss." He handed me the glass of wine, took my head in his hands, and kissed me. I realized that this had turned into date number five. This was the man that I'd come home to every night and recounted every detail of my four previous dates. This was the man who'd helped me pick out the red dress that I was to wear to Paris less than a year from that day. This same man had turned into my fifth date.

We had a wonderful night, but we both agreed that there was something missing. We were looking for that innate desire to reach out and touch someone. We longed to crave that person. We still had a great morning and he introduced me to an amazing new song to which we danced. We continued to enjoy each other as we fell against to wall kissing during our dance. At that point though, we both knew that it was just playful, and only passing fancy. We knew it lacked the undertones of the connection we were both searching for. However, he was only date number five and I said I'd go on six dates. So...

At some point that morning, he said, "You know that guy we had lunch with? I really think, although he's quiet, he has a lot going on for himself and he's really intelligent. He seems like a great guy and I think you should go out with him." I said something along the lines of, "That's funny because we have a date tonight. I guess I'll keep it"

That night, after my interview with Landmark's CEO, I met the other gentleman at a cute little cafe. We'll call him Mr. Six since he was my sixth date. We had a great time talking and decided to go for a walk up the Filbert steps to Coit Tower after dinner. We had our first kiss at the top of the stairs and then I playfully said, "Well, if I did end up moving here for this job, maybe I could live with you until I found a place." Mr. Six actually kind of said yes! I think he was wrapped up in my passion for the new position I might take on and my excitement at the idea of moving to San Francisco.

We went back to John's and caught him just as he was heading out of town to visit friends in Lake Tahoe. He seemed genuinely happy for me. That's the beauty of being open and real with people. That openness allows for a certain ease of communication. There is no need for pretense or jealousy. He could simply be happy for me and wish me the best. We could remain friends even after having shared a bit more. John gave me a hug goodbye as I would be leaving before his return.

Mr. Six and I went in and had enjoyed getting to know each other, listening to music, taking in the gorgeous view from the bay window overlooking the city lights and Bay Bridge. We spent so much time talking that we didn't realize I'd missed the last train back down to my brother's house. Mr. Six offered me a ride which was super sweet. It also meant more time to get to know one another before I left the following day. Everything happens for a reason.

The story evolved when we had a minor car accident on the way. Everybody was fine, but we were a bit shaken up after that. When we finally met up with my brother, I asked if Mr. Six could spend the night so that he didn't have to drive the hour home in a frazzled state. We ended up sleeping on a mattress together on the floor in my brother's room on our first date. Not the most romantic of endings, but a very sweet one after a long day. Also, quite a lucky one for me since my brother wouldn't seem to wake up to take me to the airport the next morning. So... thank goodness Mr. Six had spent the night because he was the one to take me to the airport.

We talked every day for the next month and sometimes for hours. At one point, I thought I hadn't gotten the job at Landmark. We spoke about my moving out there regardless of the job. I told him it would take a little time to sell things off, pack and find a different job before I moved out. I was going for it though.

However, a few short days after that I got the call from Landmark to say I had the job. The 'fun' began when they asked if I could start in a week! One challenge was that, when I arrived, Mr. Six was going to be in Switzerland working and I would need to store my items and stay somewhere else. Instead, he offered to leave the key for me. Mr. Six was leaving his home open to me. When you're focused on being open, others can be inspired to do the same.

So... three garage sales and a truckload to the Salvation Army later, I was ready to go. My aunt drove with me out to California. My car was so weighed down that the wheel wells were touching the tires when we hit big bumps. It was crazy.

Mr. Six left a key to his place at his friend's for me and I moved my stuff in while he was gone. My aunt and I went to John's house to spend the week in the city so I could walk to work my first week. John, ever the great host, gave my aunt tickets to see the Giants play the Cardinals. My aunt is a die-hard Cardinals fan so he made a great impression on her! John was off to Lake Tahoe again when we arrived and therefore was only there to say hi and give us his keys.

I finally had my second date with Mr. Six a week after my arrival in San Francisco. Upon his return from Switzerland, he picked me up from work and we went out for dinner and then 'home' together.

Less than a month later, as planned, I found a place to live with the girls at work and was getting ready to sign a lease when Mr. Six asked if I would be his roommate as his birthday present instead and I said yes. Just six months after meeting Mr. Six, he gave me a ring and as my birthday present and proposed.

Once engaged, it became clear that my schedule at work was too hectic to support our goals. We spoke of having children and I did not want to be at work all the time with kids at home. My dream was to be a stay at home mom, with an at-home career so I had an income as well. I actually started selling Juice Plus with that in mind. I hadn't worked on my Juice Plus business very hard before getting engaged though, because that dream had no deadline...until now.

We put together a plan to pay off my debt and grow my Juice Plus business. Once I reached a passive income with Juice Plus we felt would support having children, with me at home, I would quit my job and we would start our family. With this plan in place, I gave notice at Landmark Education to look for a job that would allow me the freedom to grow my Juice Plus business on the side. I would now have time to plan our wedding and the honeymoon in London and of course Paris. He had jumped on board to fulfill the Paris dream together. It's funny how things can line up to create what you want when you set an intention and share it with others.

I soon interviewed for a marketing job selling Cutco Cutlery. The funny part was that, up till that point, I couldn't tell a good knife from a bad one. The funnier part was telling the interviewer that I was recently introduced to Cutco by cutting my hand on one deep enough to warrant getting my first stitches. When I'd told my aunt I cut myself on Cutco, I found out that she was still using my grandmother's Cutco bought in 1952.

I think that these stories combined with my new free, open, playful and passionate personality got me hired. The manager later shared with me that Cutco chooses to hire people fresh out of high school or in college so they are still in the habit of being coached and trained. They know that many become set in their ways and are harder to train later on. In order to do well in any new endeavor, you need to be open to and accepting of coaching. So... I'm lucky that I'd chosen open as part of my new way of being.

This was still way out of my comfort zone. I had always been in sales or working with people, but not memorizing pages upon pages of script. They recommend practicing with people you know, but almost everyone I knew was in St. Louis and I wouldn't see them in time for my quick start. Instead of getting stuck, I choose to go door to door after showing the few people I knew in my new town. This free, open, playful and passionate person was going to make this happen and meet people in the process.

In the midst of starting with Cutco, I was planning our wedding. Just four short months after he proposed, we were married in Hawaii with our close family in attendance. Our honeymoon took place in London and yes, Paris. We were one month early to the goal of two tickets to Paris, reservations at the top of the Eiffel tower, a red dress, flowers and being with the man who loved me that I loved.

My dream of creating a family was on the horizon so I went to work. I now had my 'why' and I was working hard on hitting my passive income goal so we could start our family. Your 'why' is the real payoff. Without knowing why you're doing something or why you want it, you'll seldom get there easily.

Cutco turned out to be a great opportunity. It not only provided an immediate income but also assisted in building my Juice Plus business. I made Cutco Branch Manager in record time, won sales awards and had a great experience training and coaching my team. However, after my summer as a Branch Manager, I realized I preferred selling to hiring and training. I love being active and the more sedentary and closed up life in the office life was not for me. Going back into field sales assisted in meeting new people to continue the growth of my client base for Juice Plus. It was a fun and rewarding way to do both businesses and more in line with my goal to build Juice Plus and get ready for kids.

I joined BNI - Business Network International to promote my businesses and soon became an assistant director in the Bay Area. This provided me with an opportunity to train, coach and assist others in growing their businesses. I love training. I just didn't love being in the same office every day to do it. BNI grew my networking, presentation and sales skills exponentially which had the same effect on my income. Within two years of moving to the Bay Area, I was out of debt and well on my way to reaching my monthly passive income goal.

My Juice Plus and Cutco incomes were increasing. As I got close to the passive income goal, I stopped taking birth control to get ready to have children. However, shortly thereafter the story turns. We had already accomplished all of the goals we set forth except one. We made it to Paris, had our house and I'd paid off my debt. The next two goals were in sight. However, after I got off birth control, he admitted that he didn't feel a tug when he saw children and didn't think he should have kids unless the desire was there. I had to agree, as I didn't want to bring kids into the world without both of us feeling a committed, loving desire to have them.

This brought my career goals to a screeching halt. I had started in network marketing so I could be a stay-at-home mom and still have an income. The business I had chosen worked perfectly for stay-at-home moms because once you become a mom you interact with a completely new set of people who could use a stay at home income as well. That naturally expands your market and client base exponentially. I had also been studying nutrition and health in order to be able to take care of my children's nutritional needs and raise them to be healthy kids. None of these things mattered as much if I wasn't going to have kids.

So... I started thinking of other ways I could use the skills that I had learned and other reasons for doing the business that I had chosen. Without a 'why' though my business flatlined. Without any goals or dreams ahead of us, our relationship did as well. We had stopped working towards that common goal and hadn't created anything new to keep us moving together. Once you complete a goal, it's imperative that you create another to replace that goal. This will ensure that you always have something to strive towards that is guiding your steps and inspiring you each day. I forgot to give myself another goal so I'd have a reason to jump out of bed in the morning and bound into my life! Without a new 'why' the goals just weren't coming.

We had stopped taking any self-development classes after the second year of marriage. I now realize those classes had tied us together and given us an amazing level of communication that had our relationship work so well for the first couple years. We had lost our 'why', had few common goals and our communication was failing. Put simply, we forgot who we were. We forgot why we wanted to be together. We attempted counseling, but our dreams had diverged and without coming from our positive ways of 'being' we just couldn't put the pieces together again to see any future together. Not too long after that, we chose to divorce.

What's your 'Why'? Is it strong enough to weather the storms of life?

Life Lessons:

1. Always Be Creating-
    a. Continuously create so you have a future calling to you.
    b. Your future reminds you of who you are committed to 'be.'
    c. Your way of 'being' gives you the actions to take.
    d. The actions you take, what you 'do' constitutes your 'doing.'
    e. The actions you choose bring you the results you'll 'have.'
    f. Keep this cycle going and you will remember who you are.
2. Be Flexible-
    a. When life throws you a curve, choose your response.
    b. Choosing your response gives you a say in the matter of life.

    c. Use that space between the stimulus and your response wisely and choose a response to improves your life situation.

    d. Those moments are your opportunities to shape your future.

    e. Your response determines your level of happiness.

    f. Your response determines your direction.

    g. Your response determines your results.

3. Bounce Back-

    a. Be Open to change.

    b. Be thorough in assessing situations.

    c. Be willing to create new goals and dreams.

    d. Be strong enough to take action and move forward.

4. Know your 'why'-

    a. Your 'why' is the reason or purpose behind your actions.

    b. It will give meaning and direction to your steps each day.

    c. Your 'why' can come from or inspire your way of being.

    d. It will allow you to do all the things above when faced with the twists and turns of life.

    e. Your 'why' can change as life goes on. You may have several 'whys' that your life revolves around.

Action Steps:

1. Write down your new way of being again and come from there for these exercises.

2. What's Your 'Why'? Begin writing down ideas in your journal. Here are a few questions and an example to get you started.

    a. What keeps you going when you don't want to go?

    b. What currently gives you purpose?

    c. What inspires you in life?

    d. What calls to you?

    e. What do you want most?

    f. My 'why' is making a difference and loving my life.

        i. It gets me out of bed.

        ii. It calls to me and inspires me.

        iii. It gives me purpose and direction.

       iv. It enhances and gives my life meaning.

3. What goal or dream can you see with your new way of being and your 'why' in mind?

4. Choose a specific day in the future by which you are committed to achieving this goal. Imagine you've attained that goal. What year is it? Write down what you have on that day as if you already have it.

    a. Describe the day in the first person and present tense so that anyone reading the statement could easily see that you've achieved your desired results.

    b. What do you have now as a result of coming from the new way of being you created in the past chapter?

    c. You may be describing:

       i. A day in the place you want to visit.

       ii. A home you plan to purchase.

       iii. A day with the person you love.

       iv. A night you win an award.

       v. Or you may be going for an entirely different dream.

    d. Now that you have your results, from there, look back at the path you created over that year to lead you to this moment.

    e. What steps do you now see necessary to reach your goals?

    f. What milestones will you have reached at six months?

    g. What results can you create in the next month?

    h. What can you create this week?

5. Where else can you use this process in your life?

    a. Start making note of other goals and dreams.

    b. Write them down as you think of them daily.

    c. You'll use these to expand your list in the goals chapter.

YOU CREATE YOUR OWN UNIVERSE
AS YOU GO ALONG.

~ WINSTON CHURCHILL

YOUR IMAGINATION IS YOUR PREVIEW OF
LIFE'S COMING ATTRACTIONS.

~ ALBERT EINSTEIN

13

CHOOSE YOUR ATTITUDE

**The first look at me with truly dark brown hair - Post-divorce
Hair color courtesy of a new friend I met on a trip
who literally dyed it in the bathroom of our hostel
Montreal, Canada**

The day my ex-husband asked for a divorce, instead of wallowing in self-pity or getting angry at life, I called Landmark's San Francisco center to sign up for the next seminar. I was creating a positive support structure to assist me through this transition. Funny thing was that an old colleague answered. During our conversation, I found out two things.

1. There was a seminar starting the next day. I knew it would be great to have a group of people supporting me and would provide some positive mental training.
2. The CITO of Landmark Education was hiring for his EA. I knew and loved him. The opportunity to work as his EA was exciting as was going back to work with my Landmark family.

So... I signed up for the seminar and called world headquarters and set up an interview. Within a week I was working back in my to an office environment with the team I'd worked with before my marriage. I had added back a little bit of structure and a family to support me and replace if even just temporarily, the one I was in the process of losing.

It was perfect. I would go in every morning and talk to my boss for at least half an hour about any challenges with my divorce. He would suggest steps I could take to embrace a new life. One suggestion was to write a letter to my ex-husband. I never needed to send it, but it but it would serve to express and unsaid or lingering sentiments. This would allow me to let them go and move forward. One of the great things about working for Landmark is that they are committed to you living a life you love.

I had also built a supportive structure of friends who not only housed me while I was going through the divorce but also eventually found me a room to rent while in transition.

When I say a room, I mean that literally. My friend's ex-boyfriend had remodeled his parent's garage and added a bathroom and a storage room. This 'storage room' became my home for the next six months. No closet, no laundry, a makeshift kitchen and a shared bathroom between us. Dressers served as my closet and entertainment center. An entry table served as my desk/office. My nightstand was my filing cabinet. An end table was my kitchen. It's tiny shelves held cups, plates, and silverware with a 'mini' fridge on top. My toaster oven, Vitamix, and hot pot topped this kitchen tower. That's all I really needed. I ordered healthy fresh meals that went from fridge to toaster oven at both work and home so I didn't have a need to cook. Life was simple and it worked great.

Now, I'll tell you what made this place truly appealing. When I walked down the driveway, past the main house, here's a little taste of the vision I was greeted by each day. In between the house and my garage stood the cutest little guest cottage covered in all sorts of beautiful flowers. There was an adorable sconce lamp beside my little door and vines of beautiful flowers surrounding my entrance. As I opened to door to my little haven, I was greeted by a large California king bed draped in my favorite color of purple and framed by two sconce lights and a room painted with the softness of suede paints in a relaxing light denim blue. The 'pièce de résistance' however was a large jetted tub in the shared bathroom that I could sink into and forget any worries of the day. Did I forget to mention that my 'roommate' was a general contractor or that he had always planned for this room to be a rental not simply a storage space off of the garage?

It felt like my romantic little getaway cottage and I loved it! I loved its simplicity. I loved that it was so cute and small that I couldn't feel lost in it like I often had in my last house. Every time I came home I felt like I was being enveloped in a warm hug.

Every morning I would walk down the street to the rideshare corner and jump in someone's car for a free ride to work. The driver got a free trip over the Bay Bridge since they could use the carpool lane and the people who jumped into their car got a free ride into the city. It was a great deal. People always seem to think I'm crazy for trusting people and situations such as these, but hundreds of people do it every day and I've never heard of a crazy story related to this. So... can it really be that bad?

After my divorce, I learned to want less 'stuff'. I lived as a minimalist. There are many different schools of thought about loving your life. You can be a millionaire and want lots. You can choose to want a relaxed life and want less. The sky's the limit, but choosing what you have is a great place to start. Strive for anything but want what you have. If are not grateful for what you have that ingratitude will stunt your ability to attract more good things into your life.
The trick is to first choose to want what you have and therefore, be

happy where you are. To be happy where you are takes accepting what is. That is the pathway to gaining your heart's desire. Be grateful for what is already wonderful in your life. Besides, no amount of material items can make you happy. If you think they can, you will spend a lifetime accumulating stuff only to feel unfulfilled and move to the next desire as soon as you get the last. It is an endless cycle of emptiness.

I've learned that I can live quite simply and be completely happy. While I loved working at Landmark knowing that the company, and therefore I, was making a difference in the world, I felt it wasn't the only difference I was meant to make. You can be positively discontent or positively dissatisfied. Meaning you can be happy where you are and look at it in a positive light as I was, but still, continue to reach for your goals and dreams.

Disclaimer: To say that the difference I was making while working for Landmark was not the only difference I was meant to make does not discount the fact that I was making a profound difference in the lives of thousands of people by supporting the leadership in Landmark. I loved that about my life! However, at the same time, I knew I could achieve even more.

Several things came into play here. I knew I was meant to make a difference and I was accomplishing that goal. I also thought I was meant to make a difference by having kids and raising them to know how to take care of their health and have amazing lives to boot. I'd done so much training in health and children's nutrition and transformational education that I felt truly ready to take that on with my ex-husband. You can't control how other people may change or grow through. You can, however, control your reaction to those changes. You can choose to use the changes as a springboard into a new experience of life.

The beauty of life comes from constantly stretching yourself. When you are simply content with the way things are, you can get too comfortable and stop growing. That's why it is so important to have a future that calls you to constantly stretch yourself. This is how to stay positively discontent. You are content and growing at the same time. I love continuously learning and growing and developing myself. As my Aunt

Betty said, "It's not worth getting up in the morning if you don't learn something new."

True balance in life comes from learning to be happy where you are while at the same time working on attaining the next level. One can also get caught up in the search for meaning and thereby never truly live. You must take time in the moment to enjoy that moment fully. If you are always looking past the moment at the next you will miss so much of the beauty in life!!!!

Getting divorced was never a part of my plan. Accepting it was a huge hurdle in my life that I used to propel me forward versus cripple me. Over, under around or through, whatever it takes I'll do.

You get to choose your response in any situation. If you change your attitude you can literally change your experience of the world around you. This means that how you speak about a situation creates the story that you experience in your life related to that situation. You are the storyteller of your life. The good news here is that since you can change the way you speak about any situation, you can change the way you experience it at any time.

What hurdles do you have in your life that you are letting stop you? Who would you have to be to step over, under around or through them? Choose to live life at a higher altitude. Let's lift up your attitude to raise your altitude. After all, the view is always best from the top.

Life Lessons:

1. People don't make you happy. You make you happy.
2. Stuff doesn't make you happy. You make you happy.
3. When grey clouds of turmoil enter your life, take a new approach. You can always find a silver lining if you search for it.
4. Remember, you get what you're looking for. Look for the good in every situation and every person you meet.
5. You attract what you focus on. Focusing on the positives will help you draw amazing things into your life. So...start using

positive focus to your advantage.

Warning: Search for good, but still pay attention to possible red flags. This means to be a good finder. Follow your gut, but keep your eyes open to possibly dangerous situations. Do your due diligence.

Divorce Lessons:

1. I can handle anything!
2. I can be a minimalist.
3. I can live almost anywhere.
4. I can reinvent myself at any moment.
5. I can choose my response in any situation.
6. I can take what I'm given and create an amazing life from nothing!
7. I can be happy regardless of the circumstances in my life.
8. Accepting what is, versus getting stuck in what was, or attached to how I think it should be, is everything in life!
9. I can create powerful goals and dreams that give me purpose and call me forward into living a life I love and living it powerfully NO MATTER WHAT!
10. I can take the next step in the face of not knowing the end result. By knowing who I am and keeping my focus on my goal I can move forward. All there is to do is choose who I'm going to be in the moment and take action from that manner of being. I can be courageous, loving, accepting, adventurous or any other way of being that empowers me.

Action Steps:

1. Make a list of the great things in your life. Continue to add to it as often as possible.
2. Make lists of all the great things about the people in your life. Add to your list as often as you think of things.
3. Make a list of the great things about you and add to it as often as possible.
4. Make a list of opportunities where you see you might simplify your life to create more space for the things that matter.

5. Add to these lists as often as possible, ideally every day in your journal to continue to focus on the positive in your life to keep your attitude focused in the right direction.

ATTITUDES ARE CONTAGIOUS.
ARE YOURS WORTH CATCHING?

~ DENNIS AND WENDY MANNERING

~~~~~~

THE PESSIMIST SEES THE DIFFICULTY IN
EVERY OPPORTUNITY; AN OPTIMIST SEES
THE OPPORTUNITY IN EVERY DIFFICULTY.
POSITIVE PEOPLE DON'T JUST HAVE A GOOD
DAY; THEY MAKE IT A GOOD DAY.

~ WINSTON CHURCHILL

~~~~~~

YOUR ATTITUDE, NOT YOUR APTITUDE,
WILL DETERMINE YOUR ALTITUDE.

~ ZIG ZIGLAR

14

GET YOUR GOALS TO WORK ON YOU

Back again at my zen spot
Silver Lake, Utah

So many photos could represent your goals working on you. I'll share with you a few of my Zen spots because goals come from being focused, setting your intention and then living from there. To get focused, I think it helps to be in a quiet contemplative state. It can simply be found by closing your eyes when you want to think or by physically going somewhere. Your place might not be a place but rather a state of mind brought about by music. I created George Winston and Mozart stations on Pandora to get into a state of mind to reread and organize this book. That allowed me to focus on and enjoy the process from wherever. Find a place that brings you happiness, peace, and relaxation that allows you to reflect and work on goal setting. Yours might look like the photo of Silver Lake above, but here are a few others. Any sunset scene works for me. I can get lost in the colors.

I walked around this lake while writing a few of the chapters
Sunset over Lake Merritt- Oakland, CA

Utah sunsets are great for reflection when I write
Antelope Island, Utah

Scenes throughout Ireland and Europe inspired parts of this book
A gorgeous beach- North East Coast, Ireland

I spent time writing at many European cafes
A cute corner cafe- Lyon, France

Sunset over Seine looking back at my dance scene as I head home
Pont d'Austerlitz- Paris, France

A view of the mountains from the Ogden River Parkway
Ogden, Utah

Surround yourself with the ideas and things you love and you will see more of those start coming your way naturally. You might use tools to focus your mind on what you want. Tools such as journaling, lists, spreadsheets, vision boards or photos of places you want to visit as artwork in your home all work.

I choose to place items around my home that subliminally shift my focus onto my travel goals. My home is filled with images and artwork from or symbolizing places in France and Europe. I have several images of the Eiffel Tower and other monuments in Paris as well as a bridge from Italy and a painting that reminds me of Giverny.

I have a financial spreadsheet that I have used for several years to focus on making more than I'm spending, paying off mortgages and having my homes consistently rented so I can purchase the next home. I also mark my milestone dates on the calendar to keep goals in sight.

The specific way to focus yourself depends on your goals, your lifestyle and how you learn and assimilate information. For further assistance with setting up a system to reach your goals, I recommend finding a coach or a class that works for you. I've taken several seminars, not directly on this topic, but rather for the benefit of being around like-minded individuals also focused on accomplishing their goals. A lot can be said for surrounding yourself with people who are up to something positive in their lives.

Several of the goals I recently accomplished had their beginnings as early as grade school. Once you set an intention or goal, your mind can go to work on it behind the scenes. I have found this to be the case in several areas of my life. I considered going into architecture in high school and interior design sometime after college. I knew I wanted to do something in the area of real estate because I've always loved looking at, working on, and experiencing, new and different homes.

This all began when I was tasked by my English teacher to design a room in a house. The assignment had me describe the room and I also drew it out. A bathroom was the only room where I could settle on just one style. Every time I thought of designing another room type I wanted to incorporate too many different styles. I've chosen a few of my homes based on this bathroom I designed in school. It became one of the goals that began working on me in my subconscious.

My mother bought renovated and rented houses as I was growing up. She also at one point owned a few apartment complexes. For this reason, I've always been drawn to real estate. I've also always liked a wide variety of architectural styles and interior design concepts ranging from loft apartments to Victorians with white picket fences. When I was married and working for Cutco I was in new homes every week and sometimes I would walk through the model homes in the neighborhoods my clients lived in just to see the decor and different architectural designs. It was then that I designed the interior for my dream home in my mind. I will create this after retiring. At the time of writing this book, I'm almost there!

I used to think about buying a different house for each style: one by the beach, one by a lake, one in the city, one in the mountains, etc. I thought it would be great to have houses that had a place that would allow a manager to live onsite and possibly maintain it as a bed and breakfast. That may still happen, but it's not my current focus. It's good to set dreams that call you into a bigger future as I did with Paris.

I moved to Utah to invest in real estate after my divorce. I've taken real estate investing and self-development courses requiring a lot of travel which was expensive. By investing in my future I found myself in debt again, but for a great cause. Education! I also created a plan in place to get out of debt.

I met someone in one of my courses who introduced me to an investor named Shawn, who had researched the Utah real estate market. It was quite serendipitous. I had looked into several foreclosure markets, but Utah's was the first and last I visited. Funny side note; when my aunt and I drove together on my move to San Francisco I remember passing Salt Lake City and stopping to take a photo by the Great Salt Lake. It was July which meant the lake stunk of sulfur and there were brine flies all around. I took a photo holding my nose to remember never to come back. At the time of writing this book, I'd lived in Utah for ten years. Never say never.

The second time I visited Utah, just like my second time visiting California, I fell in love. The mountains and the Mayor's plan to build up Ogden, Utah called to me. I also loved the idea of working with a mentor like Shawn. In two short days, he showed me the Mayor's plan as well as the current conditions. He made sure to show me the good, the bad and the ugly. He also set me up to live with his contractor Ryan, who had a room for rent. Ryan wasn't in town to show me the room, but in speaking with him over the phone I got a good feeling about him. Shawn and I drove by his house in a cute, convenient neighborhood where I could see myself living.

Everything was falling into place perfectly. So... and I chose to take a leap. I left a suitcase and deposit for Ryan and shipped everything to him without ever meeting him or seeing the room. When I arrived a month later, he had unpacked the containers I'd shipped so that they could ship back right away saving me from paying extra. He also moved me into the master suite versus the guest room so I wouldn't have to walk across the hall to the bathroom. He was so wonderfully respectful that I knew I'd made the right choice.

After moving to Utah, Shawn said other investors had simply given him $10,000 to invest in his flipping projects. I hadn't taken investing courses to give someone else my money and do nothing. I wanted to experience working with a mentor. Since this was my intent, we parted ways and I looked into flipping houses by myself. After placing about 100 offers with a zero acceptance rate, I changed my strategy. To me, flipping was stressful. I was raised with rental properties in my blood. The idea of buying houses and having to borrow money at high hard money interest rates, then renovate in the hopes that it would sell at the price I wanted, made me nervous. I was starting out right before the downturn of the real estate market, so thank goodness none of my offers were accepted and I didn't give him my money to invest. That was the universe watching out for me. Many of my friends lost everything flipping houses or buying spec homes that went down in value versus up.

So... I am glad I trusted my gut back then and went my own way. I may have made a little bit more money or lost it all, but either way, my quality of life wouldn't have been as wonderful. I chose to do it slow and steady like my mom and it's worked well for me. Some friends have used the fast and furious method and it worked for them. It's all based on your desires and where you choose to place your focus. No one plan works for everyone. In any endeavor, it's important to trust your gut and go with what works for you.

My investing courses taught me how to buy without a realtor to save money. I also learned how to use lease-to-own options which allowed me the needed time to build up my self-employment income and sufficient payment history to qualify for a decent loan. If I had gotten a loan right off the bat, my interest rate would have been awful since I was in debt from the investing courses. After a year I was able to finance my first property without problems.

My first renter happened naturally when my new chiropractor found out that my condo was 5 minutes from his office. He knew my goal was to eventually rent the condo so he got excited and talked me into moving closer to my work so he could move closer to his office. By sharing my goals I had set myself up to win. When you set and share your goals it's fun to watch the universe line things up to bring them to life.

I was now renting five minutes from my work. I still had a pool and walking path, which were features of the condo I'd purchased, but now I also had a hot tub and more interesting neighbors. When I got upgraded to a two bedroom place due to a mold situation, I was able to take in a roommate for a few months. This allowed me to pay off my real estate investing courses more quickly! After just over a year I was ready to buy my next house.

In December of 2011, I finalized the purchase of a great townhouse with granite countertops, sleek black appliances, and a cute little patio. The inside was a nice upgrade compared to my first property.

I was still close to the running paths by the river but sadly, this one didn't have a pool or hot tub.

I had a few stumbling blocks during this purchase because it was a short sale. This meant the loan took much longer than expected to close. So... I ended up moving all my belonging into storage with my best friend's help. We left for  my mom's house in Santa Cruz the next day on a girl's road trip for Thanksgiving. I didn't get to move into my new home until a day or so before I had planned on leaving town to go to St. Louis for Christmas.

This meant I lived with my best friend for a month. She was and continues to be Godsend! My friends and family have been my rocks in life. They have given me stability to be able to take all of the crazy leaps of faith I've taken. My friends say they live vicariously through me with all of my crazy adventures. I have found that I live vicariously through them watching their kids grow up.

Not long after buying this townhome, I got engaged again and I moved into his home. However, I quickly realized that we weren't going to work and moved out less than a year later. Ironically, I moved back into the same apartment complex that I lived in before. Some would say this was unfortunate, but it's all about perception. Here's a great example of my view of life. I put my spin on this as I do everything. I choose to look at the positive. First, regarding moving back into the same complex, some might say that was a step back. I see it as a step forward. I had to take a year or two between home purchases anyway in order to establish rental income history to offset the mortgage payment I was making. Also, this time, I knew exactly what I wanted when I moved into the complex and it was like moving home. Something familiar is always great after a breakup. It gave me a sense of stability in what could have been considered chaos. I moved to the top floor so no one would be stomping around making noise above me. I had a better view and a fireplace. I also liked the extra exercise I got from being on the top floor.

My relationship with my ex-fiancé showed me the things I wanted to look for in my next relationship. The situation also allowed me the opportunity to rent out the most recent condo and begin building the rental income history for my next home purchase. (In order to count rental income against mortgage payments when buying homes, you have to wait till the income is shown on two years of tax returns.) The time spent at his home allowed me to claim the rental income for one more year. When combined with renting that next year, I was set up to buy again. It was a win-win for both of us because I was paying half his mortgage out of my rental income. It also allowed me to experience living with someone again so I didn't get so set in my ways that I couldn't adapt when I found the right guy. There were many other positives, but I just wanted to give you an idea of how to focus on the positive when you hit what could otherwise be seen as a setback in life.

At the end of my year renting this time, I thought I was ready to buy another property. I found a couple places and went to my mortgage broker to plan it out. That's when I realized I wasn't ready. This was one of the stumbling blocks that I turned into a stepping stone. My lease was up in August and I had filed an extension on my taxes. I didn't think about the fact that I had to actually file my taxes before I could get a loan. At this point, I couldn't file before I needed to move. You may not be interested in purchasing real estate, and therefore, these details may seem superfluous. They are included to show the need for research to attain your goals. With that said, I was dealing with a few roadblocks. My lease was up and I didn't want to pay month to month pricing for the next few months while waiting for my tax return to show my income for the loan. I also didn't want to move my stuff twice as I had the last time.

Instead of stopping in my pursuit to purchase a home, I shifted my focus to homes where the owners would allow me to set up a lease-to-own situation. Over, under, around or through, whatever it takes, I'll do! I love that saying and I repeat it often when hitting roadblocks in life. It helps me refocus and find another option to accomplish my objective. Many times I share details to show how things happen just at the right time and seem to flow seamlessly from one goal to the next falling into place perfectly.

I found both a home and a condo whose owners were willing to work with me. After creating a list of positives and negatives about each, I chose the condo. I am so glad I chose the condo in hindsight. It was easier to manage a $50,000 purchase. It caused me to jump through a few more hoops, but not managing a yard or $120,000 mortgage on the home was a better fit for my life. I also lived closer to work, a running trail, my gym and still had a pool, but no hot tub.

Shortly after I bought this rental I got a promotion to a hotel south of Salt Lake. I was interested in moving closer to work again. I also had an interest in living in or near the city for a change of pace and a new adventure. So...I got a renter for my place and found the great rental just a mile from my work. I was able to negotiate an open-ended lease agreement so that I was free to buy a place in the first six months if I found one I liked. I had also created an opening for a move or to fulfill my dreams and goals elsewhere if this position didn't work out. Just 8 eight months after I was offered a huge raise to take a position opening a new hotel back up north. Thankfully, I'd prepared and was able to use that open-ended lease and move yet again! There is more to this story but I will save that for the last chapter.

After settling in with the new company I found the perfect townhome about a mile away. Amazing how that seems to happen, isn't it? Funny thing is that this home was the first one I saw when I started looking in and it's the home I eventually bought. I looked at several others, but this first home was to one for me.

When I moved to Utah I'd looked at homes in that complex, but at that time there was literally nothing more than a gas station and grocery store near the development. If I'd had the money it would've been a fun home at that time. However, I didn't and that worked to my advantage as seems to be the case. This home which only gained went up $10,000 in 10 years jumped by over $30,000 in the 2 short years I owned it. So... it seems I invested at just the right time.

The other reason this turned out to be the right time is that I realized that I couldn't use this as a long-term rental. I asked this question of the HOA at the time of purchase but was given misinformation. (Lesson: Get it in writing.) However, that just means I got to sell at a nice profit and reinvest that gain into other homes. What could have been seen as a stumbling block was again turned into a stepping stone and used to reach my next chapter in life. All signs pointed to a positive outcome.

We all choose our battles and I would rather have an HOA than deal with hiring a gardener or having to deal with the cost of a roof, etc. I've therefore always chosen to purchase condos or townhomes versus single family homes. In my world, it makes my life easier. Up to this point, I've chosen to manage all of my own properties using various online tools and it's been quite easy. Given that my focus has been to find good renters, very few renters have cause any problems and when they have it's been minor and I've used it as a lesson. Remember, from previous chapters, you find what you're looking for. I've found carefree, high return, positive situations.

Life Lessons:

1. Share your goals; get the universe working for you.
2. Do your due diligence when planning for your goals.
3. Figure out how you work best and play to your strengths.
4. Go with your gut. Do what feels right to you.
5. Find and use strategies that work for you.
6. Choose your battles.
7. Get it in writing.

Action Steps:

1. Make a list of all the goals you've achieved in your life.
2. Make a list of the goals you are working on.
3. Make a list of your dreams.

4. Give them each a deadline or date by which you'll complete them.
5. Now look back and follow the steps from chapter twelve for each to create milestones with a timeline for each goal you've listed.
6. Now that they're in your mind, let them go to work on you! Your subconscious can now assist you in bringing about what you are thinking about!
7. Get into action! It has been said by some that the Lord helps those who help themselves. You must act on as well as think about your goals.

IF YOU CAN DREAM IT,
YOU CAN DO IT.

~ WALT DISNEY

15

CELEBRATE YOUR WINS

**On a cruise ship celebrating my wins
Somewhere, Caribbean Sea**

Let's step back in time a bit and talk about celebrating some of the wins I achieved in the last chapter. I had several reasons for starting in the hotel business. The first and most obvious was a plan to get out of debt within five years. The other underlying reasons were less obvious. I missed working with a team all day and having someone to bounce ideas off of and even someone to help guide my steps. The other reason had to do with image. I liked the idea of the image prestige of the title that working for someone else gave me.

When I sold Juice Plus full time, the focus on nutrition assisted me in my own focus on taking care of my health and my body. However, I shifted to hotels with a plan; to get out of debt within 5 years. This plan had me become focused on that plan above all others and I allowed my wellbeing to deteriorate slowly. For example, when attending work events, I would eat whatever was served since it was free, even if it meant eating something that wasn't healthy. Over the course of the next 5 years as my debt went down, my weight inched up. I had the wherewithal to keep it from going too far and I still made healthy choices at home and hit to the gym or went running or hiking with friends. However, I allowed the foods I had avoided successfully for years, that I knew weren't good for me, to creep back into my diet. Then I would try quick fixes to lose weight which are never a good idea. I achieved my goal of getting out of debt, but at what cost?

Balance is also important in life and it's a delicate art as they say. I planned a cruise to celebrate my win after completing my objective on time. Not only had I eliminated the debt through working hard. I'd also accumulated 3 rental properties by applying my real estate investing education. This was perfect timing to create short-term goal or milestone for the game of regaining my health. I planned a cruise as a reward for my efforts, then lost 15 pounds that month and had a great time celebrating my win with my college friend and her husband on the cruise. We met a crazy group of people and had an insane amount of fun.

While enjoying the island of Saint Thomas I decided to go shopping. I found a set of jewelry that I had been 'wanting' for almost 20 years. Back when I first saw tanzanite on the home shopping network, I said I can't afford that right now, but when I have money I'm going to get a trillion cut tanzanite and opal ring. I found just that, along with a set of trillion cut earrings and a beautiful matching necklace.

This was my 'I have arrived' set of jewelry. It was a wonderful feeling to know that I could finally afford it and deserved it. Delayed gratification feels great!

When I came back from the cruise, I began planning my next trip to celebrate having attained the three rental units I'd planned to attain by this time. I have always wanted to live in France for a few months to become more fluent in French and see what it's like to live as a Parisian. Allow me to give you a bit more background as to why.

When I was in junior high my dad said that if I studied French for two years he would take me to France for my junior high graduation, so of course, I said yes and began studying. I was only 12 when I went to France for the first time. We stayed in Europe for two weeks. We landed in Germany, but only stayed one night. We headed straight to France staying in Paris first then the French Riviera. When we went to Switzerland we stayed in the Alps and traveled through Geneva, Lausanne, and Zürich. We got to see the last through a local's eyes while staying with my father's friends.

His challenge to learn French and our European excursion caused me to fall in love with France, Europe and speaking French. I continued to study the language for thirteen years, all through college including a summer away for an immersion course in Quebec at Laval University. *Incroyable!*

This is when I got the idea that spending a summer living like a local in Paris would be a great experience. I worked for TGI Friday's in college and had worked with my professor to practice for an interview at their Paris location. For graduation from college, my mom was taking me on a trip to Europe. My plan was to interview with them during the trip and spend the summer working in Paris after my family left. However, I let my interaction with the TGI Friday's manager stop me. We didn't click and I didn't want to spend a summer working with him. So... all of these years later that goal was still working on me in the back of my mind. I was still thinking *How in the world can I arrange three months off work and still afford to live in France?*

With this in mind, I realized that over the 5 years with my company I had accrued a month vacation, it wasn't the three months I was hoping for but it would still be enough time to offer the experience of living like a local. I was hoping to not only live out a smaller version of my dream but also keep my career. I loved working in the hospitality industry and I loved my clients and my team. I worked a ton and although I still had loads of fun in my off time, the work took a toll.

When I realized I wasn't going to get at least a month-long Paris vacation, I started again to think *How I can create my dream of living in Paris for a summer?* It was becoming clear that I may need to look at working for myself again. As I said in the last chapter, once you put dreams and ideas out there, your mind, sometimes unbeknownst to you, starts creating them in the background. Mine had been doing just that for over fifteen years at this point. I had thought of several scenarios over the years, but I hadn't discovered one that I thought would truly work, at that time. Therefore, I chose to accept what I had been given and planned a two and a half week vacation at the end of September.

I planned to stay in Paris and then visit my friend in Belgium for a few days so I could add a new country to my list. The trip was absolutely perfect. I stayed in Paris for free most of the time and at a discount the rest of the time because of my hotel connections. The day I arrived I was able to relax in a gorgeous Courtyard by Marriott. I recuperated from the flight just enough to go out dancing the rest of the night.

However, on my way home I got lost in the metro and missed the last train after having taken the wrong train twice. It was only a couple of miles to the hotel and I was no stranger to walking, so I set out in that direction. I had just passed two 'ladies-of-the-night' and was at a huge intersection trying to find my way when a lovely man started walking toward me.

He had the sweetest smile on his face and looked like heaven in his three-piece suit. I asked which way I should go to get to Saint-Denis. To this, he replied "Tu ne veux pas y aller à cette heure à pied. C'est trop dangereux." Translation- You don't want to go there at this hour by foot. It's too dangerous. He then continued in French, "Let me give you a ride my car is just down the street." I looked at him questioningly, but I've always had a good sense about people and he looked trustworthy. We chatted a bit more and, as crazy as it seems, I let him drive me back to the hotel. We shared an amazing kiss goodnight outside in the car and I headed up to my room. We saw each other several times during the course of my time in Paris. He made a great tour guide and made my time in Paris much more enjoyable.

I spent the next few days wandering the streets of this city I'd fallen in love with and staying with people that I hadn't met till arriving at their doors. Couch surfing is an amazing thing. I got so lucky in finding such generous hosts. My first host took me on a bike tour around the Bois de Vincennes. He owned the bar just a block from his house and we danced salsa while drinking mojitos.

I decided the best way to learn French was to be around as many French people as possible. So... I chose to create a profile on a dating website to meet people to see the city with and to assist in improving my French. I went for a motorcycle tour of the Champs-Élysées and the Bois de Boulogne. I walked along the seine at night stopping for a drink in a cute cafe right outside Place de la Bastille. I also had a coffee at La Défense with a French police officer who I fell for instantly. Unfortunately, he realized his heart already belonged to someone else.

I also had my first experience with someone picking me up on the streets of France. I heard someone saying "Bonjour, bonjour madame," "Hello, hello miss." He stopped me and after a series of compliments and questions, he asked to carry my bags so he could talk to me all the way up the street to my host's home. He then asked if he could take me to lunch. We ended up spending the entire day together and he was quite sweet, but when we kissed goodbye I felt nothing and knew it wasn't meant to be.

Visiting my friend Stef in Belgium was the biggest surprise of my trip. He lived just outside Bruges and took me all over the city. We went to an interesting exhibit that went through the town's history with holographic stories set back in time. We stood in the bell tower where Colin Farrell stood in the movie *En Bruges*. We visited the Madonna featured in the movie *Monuments Men*. Little did I know that the best was yet to come.

The next day we drove to Ghent where Stef enlisted the help of his friend Max of the Belgian Royal Air Force. Since Max was from Ghent he knew a great deal about its history, including intricate details that only a tour guide would know. He was able to take us on a journey through the gorgeous little town complete with a gondola ride and a stop at his family's cafe for coffee and homemade pastries. It was the perfect afternoon break. We visited the town's shops and he gifted me with their delicacies. I received mustard and relish made on site and stored in huge barrels below one shop. He purchased nozen (sweet, cone-shaped, raspberry filled candies) from street vendors vying for our business. Max and Stef then fought over who purchased lunch and I was left to simply enjoy the day. It was absolutely divine. I had two men, one for each arm, buying me gifts, treating me to lunch and unveiling the beautiful town in front of me. What more could a woman ask for?

Saying goodbye to Max that day was bittersweet because even though I was sad to leave, I now knew I had a new friend to visit in Belgium. Stef and I returned to Bruges. We took a carriage ride through town the next day enjoying beautiful canals while listening to the driver recount stories of the city. My Belgian weekend was topped off with a run through the picturesque countryside by cute cottages and a little chateau with Steph, and his family. What a weekend.

When I returned to Paris, I had little more than a day to enjoy the sites before leaving. So... I took full advantage. My Brazilian friend Luis, from my first night in Paris, took me out for dinner and karaoke. The truly unreal part of this trip was that it was only a drop in the bucket compared to what was to come and it whetted my appetite in anticipation and preparation.

When you celebrate your wins, it helps you get excited about completing your next objective or reaching that next peak. The cruise, the set of jewelry and mini European vacation were all celebrations of my achievements. The last also assisted me in the planning needed to reach my true objective, the ultimate European adventure.

Life Lessons:

1. Taking time to celebrate your wins has several benefits.
    a. It reminds you to feel good about your achievements.
    b. It gives you a reward to look forward to attaining goals.
    c. It can also assist in planning your next goal as in my case.
2. Turn your stumbling blocks into stepping stones that you can stand on to reach your goals.
3. Delayed gratification feels amazing.

Action Steps:

1. Write down possible rewards or celebrations for reaching goals in your life:
    a. List a few little ones that don't require much to produce.
        i. A massage
        ii. A night out with friends to celebrate
        iii. A simple walk in the park to enjoy the sunset
        iv. Anything you've wanted to do or to acquire but haven't spent the money or time to acquire or enjoy.
    b. Create a few that would be a worthy celebration for big goals.
        i. A vacation like mine
        ii. An expensive accessory like a watch or set of jewelry, a suit or dress or perhaps a whole new wardrobe
        iii. Any large purchases you've put off till now

THE MORE YOU CELEBRATE YOUR LIFE,
THE MORE THERE IS TO CELEBRATE IN LIFE.

~ OPRAH WINFREY

16

STEPPING STONES TO EUROPE

**Taken by my friend Max during my mini Europe trip
Ghent, Belgium**

Upon my return from two weeks abroad, I realized that I wanted more time in France. In my twenties, I dreamt of backpacking through Europe, but now I realized that a roller bag would be much more conducive to the type of travel I that interested me.

I started to take a new look at my life at that point and reevaluate what was important to me. While I enjoyed hotels and my clients, my main complaint was that I couldn't see this career path allowing me to make the difference I was committed to making in the world. I could see how I made a difference in the lives of my guests and clients and it definitely served its intended purpose of getting me out of debt and into investment properties. However, I knew I could now expand my ability to make a difference in the world further somewhere else.

Some people make their difference through service, some through creating amazing things and some through leading others to fulfill their purpose. Others make a difference in the small things they do every day. People can also make a difference in grand gestures. Everyone can leave their mark. It's up to each person to decide how.

I now knew that working for hotels was most likely not my end game. It didn't seem to be the only mark I was meant to leave on the world long term. I absolutely love learning and growing as a person, fulfilling dreams and achieving goals. I accomplished all of these things during my time in hospitality. It was rich in experiences that served me and those around me well for my having been there. Everything has its place and its time and I was realizing my time in the hospitality industry might need to come to an end. I wanted a career that allowed me the freedom to travel, not just a discount when I chose to travel. I also wanted a career that allowed me to touch more lives in a positive way.

However, I still hadn't achieved the one goal in hospitality that I had been craving for a couple of years. I realized I hadn't been given a new hotel to open. I was so new in the industry that I had been turned down for a promotion to open a new hotel. Ironically, my promotion to the South Salt Lake hotel was due to the fact that the person they hired instead hadn't worked out. I had been able to come in where they left off and make it profitable. Knowing that they now saw me as ready, less than a year later, was a huge compliment. I also now had a new success on my resume.

Given my uncertainty about staying in my career in hospitality, I considered quitting my job and traveling the following summer. I was set up in the perfect situation with all of my homes rented and, if you remember, I had a lease that I could get out of at a month's notice. So... I told myself *if I'm not in a serious relationship by April I'm out of here and headed to Europe.* I planned to take the summer to fulfill my dream and create a future to live into that made a difference.

Then what happens? I meet someone who's really great and we start dating. Around that same time, a hotel client of mine called me to say he'd like to recommend me to a company opening a new Hyatt Place hotel in a development next to his work called Station Park. It was a gorgeous shopping complex and just happened to be one of my favorite places. There were tons of restaurants, great shops, a movie theater and a beautifully animated fountain in the center. The raise that this new company offered me was above yet another goal I'd set and yet to achieve. In other words, it was way too good to pass up. Not to mention, this was my opportunity to fulfill my goal of opening a new hotel and a Hyatt Place no less. It seemed the universe was giving me just what I'd asked for and I decided Europe could wait.

The owners that we were working for were wonderful. The company I worked for was supportive and the benefits were great as was the salary. Everything looked perfect. I started the job just a few days before my birthday in December and before the company Christmas party. That group of people knew how to have fun! We went out to Station Park's little ice skating rink after a dinner party next door at the martini bar. It was hilarious to watch I'm sure. I ended up flat on my back at one point when my feet slipped right out from under me. It was hilarious since I wasn't even drunk. I guess that's why they call it being tipsy though.

At that point, I lived a long way from work. This and many other factors prompted me to start looking for houses in the area. The first house I saw was in the complex where I had wanted to buy when I first moved to Utah. It had an amazing open floor plan with a cathedral ceiling over the entryway and a great view of the mountains. The humongous master bedroom came complete with a sumptuous master bath boasting a soaking tub, separate shower and walk-in closet. I looked at other places, but I think in my mind's eye I was set on that one from the start. I was able to, as in the past, work with the owner to postpone the purchase till I could ready the funds. Just four months after starting my new position I had moved into my dream townhouse in Utah.

However, after these few months with the great man I met, it became clear that we were more friends than lovers. By the time I realized this however, I was too deep in my new position. I was smack dab in the middle of opening a hotel. My deadline for leaving had already passed and I had already moved into a new position and a new home. I wasn't about to abandon ship now. I had too much on the line and I was committed to a successful opening.

Everything happens for a reason. I realized that because of the raise, I had been able to pay off a large portion of the last condo I'd purchased. As I continued down the path of opening this hotel and the stress rose and the deadlines came and went and success loomed in the foreground it became clear that although I knew I could be successful in the hotel business it still wasn't fulfilling my passion and purpose.

We had had some major upheavals in the hotel though as the sales manager took on the assistant general manager position and I was left alone for the month of October, which was crazy busy with events. We had our biggest month ever in events and I ran it by myself.

It was during this crazy month that I began planning my retreat from the world of hospitality. I set my sights on fulfilling my twenty-year dream of living in France for a summer. I even upgraded that dream to include at least a month of traveling around Europe so that I could combine those two dreams into one amazing adventure.

By November I had hired a great new sales coordinator and began training Jordan. In December I found out that I had developed fibroids in my uterus which made it all the more clear that it was time to leave the stress of hotel sales. By this time Jordan was trained and ready to move into his own office and we were a great team for the month of January and February until I was finally ready to leave. I wanted to wait until I knew he was ready to be there is the support structure for whoever came in as the new Director of Sales.

Since the crazy month of October, I'd been doing my research and realized that I could get by without the income from my hotel position.

The beautiful thing about the universe is that once you set a goal and start taking action, it assists you in fulfilling that goal. Note: In order for goals to work on you in the background of life you must believe they are attainable. The universe will give you evidence for any point of view you choose. So... stay positive. Keep the faith and stay focused in the direction you want to go and the universe will say yes to your goals.

The universe started putting the necessary things in my path to get me where I needed to be in order to comfortably quit my job by the end of February. I started setting up my second bedroom so to list on Airbnb. Then I realized that my HOA rules prevented me from doing Airbnb. It was then that I chose to look for a roommate. When one door closes a window opens. Remaining open-minded with a positive focus also allows the universe to show you other ways to attain your goals. I found the perfect roommate who just happened to want to move in the day after I quit my job. Everything was lining up and she was perfectly fine with the knowledge that I would be renting out my room as well within the next few months so that I could leave for France.

I spent the next month planning my trip to France and looking for the second roommate who showed up not only just in time but early. She moved in, but let me stay there as well since the move in was unplanned and we shared the space for a week or so before I left.

The money she provided, paid for the tests that I needed to determine the severity of my fibroids. I had chosen I could manage my fibroids without surgery. I chose not to take the medications they suggested since they all had awful side effects that could inhibit my ability to have children. I was not willing to relinquish that dream. Instead, I started to look for natural remedies.

The other amazing thing that happened shortly after my last day, was a friend of mine posted a position as and in turn at her online publishing company. Given that my plan was to write a book within the next year I thought this was a perfect opportunity. However, I wasn't sure if she would be okay with someone working from Europe. I quickly gave her a call and after a quick conversation, it was clear that this was something that I could do while traveling.

We planned to meet and do training before I left so that I could work on the road. All the pieces were falling into place I had rent out my house to cover my mortgage I even rented out my car to cover my car payment and I'd found a job that would allow me to work while traveling. It really is true that you get what you're looking for. I knew that everything would work out and I trusted that if I took the steps necessary to get the ball rolling and continually focused on my goal in what I wanted the right things would come my way. I this trend happened not just before my trip but during and after.

When I looked back at the goals I set for myself before moving to Utah, I realized that I'd accomplished almost all of them. I had said that I wanted five rental units and I now had five renters. Not including my car which makes six. I only had four homes so far, but one of those homes was rented to two different people. I had paid off all of my debt from traveling after my divorce and taking real estate investing courses and buying a new car. My last position had the annual salary goal I'd set to earn working for someone else. I attained the goal of opening a hotel. I even moved into the house that I wanted when I arrived in Utah. I had a walking path, hot tub, pool and fitness center all on site.

However, these were all monetary goals and while they improved my quality of life, it was time to fulfill some personal development goals. I wanted to reconnect with my purpose again and stay living true to myself. Funny thing was, as soon as I quit my job impact training had a course coming up the following weekend. It was time to go back and complete the courses at Impact Training that follow the initial Quest training. I postponed my Europe departure by a month to complete the entire program.

Everything happened just right yet again. In the last class, I met a girl who was also planning to go to Ireland which was one of the places on my bucket list. We had talked during the courses but only discovered this when we were paired to share something we were truly passionate about. The funny thing was we were both passionate about a trip we were taking that summer. We connected at such a deep level that we decided to meet up in Ireland. I was now going to go on part of the trip with her and her friend. Even the airlines had aligned to make it happen.

The cheapest ticket I found just happened to land in Dublin on the same day she arrived. How's that for the law of attraction?

Since this dream was settled in the back of my mind, my short trip to Paris and Belgium became a test run and stepping stone to my true European vacation. I stayed with people and traveled super cheap. I found a great rate on the flight and stayed for free aside from two nights. As a result of all of this, I was able to tell myself, OK. I can do this I made enough money at the last job before the trip to pay off all but my car and the mortgages. I had a positive cash flow from my homes. That meant I wouldn't need to earn too much extra while away especially if I rented out my car. I also had the internship with Elite Online Publishing to help with spending money. My only extra expenditure would be the flight, traveling between cities and any hostels or hotels. I was set. Everything was coming together perfectly in my mind and in reality. It all started with a vision in seventh grade with my dad's challenge to take French, built upon by a summer in Quebec studying French and my college graduation trip where I interviewed to work there for the summer. It was cemented in place by my two-week trip two years prior. It wasn't overnight, but it happened and at the perfect time!

I planned it out, rented both of the rooms in my house out to two separate people and my car. Everything fell into place. I met a girl in the class that I'd been taking that was also going to Ireland and several other things lined up as well. Several of the friends that I've made over the years had said I could visit and stay with them. Even a client from one of the hotels I worked for invited me to stay with him. This gentleman had stayed at the hotel with us for three months. I found a gentleman in Paris that offered me a place to stay for three months. Even though that didn't pan out because after a month he got a girlfriend and she didn't like that I was there, it was perfect. I decided to move out he gave me a few days to find a place and I stayed in a hostel for a few days in Paris where I met the girl from Russia that was going to Nice. I met all kinds of people that I still am in contact with and I'm probably going to go to Russia next time I visit to visit her and these two other people I met there. I met a great group of people and celebrated Bastille Day with them watching fireworks at the Eiffel Tower. What a great night!!!

The girls that I met in Ireland at the start of my trip were probably the best influence. I planned trips to visit them. While traveling, an old work colleague asked if I was going to Croatia saying it was on their bucket list. I wasn't even planning on Croatia. I met a girl in Dublin, who was originally from Croatia. She invited me to stay with her in Munich and while there she heartily recommended I visit Croatia. She's from there and had just recently moved to Munich and raved about her home country. Also in Ireland, I met Lydia, who I stayed with later in Vienna she also mentioned that she loved Croatia.

After so many signs, I decided to go to Croatia. Before heading south though Lydia and I met Prague for a fun weekend. She'd shared her love for Prague with me during my visit with her in Vienna and planned to show me around the city. We stayed up till 6 am dancing after a full day of sightseeing! What a great weekend!

Following my gut after Prague, I went to Budapest then Croatia. While in Croatia I met another girl from Munich who invited me back for Oktoberfest. Lydia planned to meet me there as well. However, it came up in conversation that neither Lydia nor I had been to Salzburg so we changed plans and she met me in Salzburg. We explored all day that then stayed out until 6 am again dancing and meeting new friends in pubs around town. She was literally half my age and I loved being able to keep up with her. It didn't hurt that the guys her age were hitting on me thinking I was only a few years older than her.

I think one of the most magical moments was dancing on the Seine almost every night of the week in Paris. All along the seine, there are bars right along the little walking path. In some cases, you dance right in the path while bikes walkers, police officers on horseback and others are going right along their way. You can also choose to ride bikes and then there's like little parks and other fun things along the Seine and during this summer they just have the dancers all over. They had a live band at the Lindy Hop night I attended. That was awesome. They all danced a fun Lindy hop line dance. I did it with them the next time I saw it, but I don't really think it was the same dance, but I was recording it the first time so I didn't dance it. Next summer I plan to go back and try it again.

On this European adventure, I didn't even go inside the monuments in Paris unless I was with friends. I had already seen them on my previous visits so instead, I made an effort to take a tour of as many of the parks as I could. Exploring the streets to take in the architecture and parks was my favorite thing.

Do you find yourself getting stuck doing what others think is important? Have you been doing what you thought you 'should'? Have you been living someone else's dream for you or worse for them? It's time to follow your own inspiration. Find what lights you up and do it. Create your own dreams. I loved getting lost in the streets of Paris. I loved finding new places to go dancing in Paris. I loved finding gorgeous photo opportunities. What do you love? Take advantage of every opportunity to enjoy those things you love. In doing so you'll create so opportunities to grow the love in your life.

Life Lessons:

1. If you stumble on your stepping stones you can use those stumbling blocks to build a staircase to reach your next goal.
2. Turn your challenges into growth opportunities.
3. Look for life to help you along and it will.
4. Listen to your heart.
5. Enjoy the Journey.
6. Live your dreams.
7. Go with the flow.
8. Fail forward.

Action Steps:

1. Where in your life are you facing challenges?
2. How can you reframe these challenges as opportunities?
3. Describe a time you felt like everything went your way.
   a. How did it feel?
   b. What mindset did you have leading up to it?
   c. Were you thinking everything would work out?
4. Look back and make a list of the times that life has given you a

helping hand.

5. Keep reframing challenges and growing to reach your goals. Soon you'll begin to naturally think from this winning attitude.

6. Look now and list challenges you see to learn and grow from.

7. What challenges can you step up on to reach your next goal?
    a. Look at your list of goals from chapter fourteen.
    b. List challenges you see that you may face.
    c. Now list ways you can overcome these!

8. Continue to grow and work on you. Growth is a never-ending process. You can always learn. Kaisen = Constant and never-ending improvement. Remember, you are either growing or you are dying.

9. Start loving your life now! Take action and go back through the lessons and actions steps in the book. I've summarized them in this next chapter. This will make it easy to refer back for a quick lesson or so you can continue to update your answers as your life changes. If you'd like even more support in taking action you can purchase the journal or workbook at www.ILoveMyselfSo.com

10. **Quick Summary**
    a. Refer back to this book whenever you have a challenge. Read the chapter that applies to that challenge and it will remind you what to do in the moment.
    b. Listen to your heart and focus on what you truly desire and allow it to begin to come to you naturally.
    c. Remember, that what drives you in any given moment may change. In order to move forward, it works best to go with the flow and accept that change is a part of life.
    d. Embrace your perfect imperfection and accept the assistance when need. Be it from family, a friend or a coach of some sort.
    e. Share what you've learned with the world. In sharing what you have learned you understand at a deeper level. In sharing you get to grow and develop yourself! It's the gift that gives back!
    f. **What will you do right now coming from truly loving yourself?**

Go Do It!!! Go Create A Life You Love!!!!

Take the first step in faith. You don't
have to see the whole staircase.
Just take the first step.

~ Dr. Martin Luther King Jr.

TURN YOUR STUMBLING BLOCKS INTO
STEPPING STONES TO REACH YOUR DREAMS

~ CORY JENKINS

17

TAKE ACTION
Summary

In this chapter, I've pulled together all of the life lessons and action steps from each chapter to make it easier for you to take actions in your life that open you up to living a life you love right now. It's all about choice. In every experience, you can choose to see a roadblock or an opportunity; a stumbling block or a stepping stone; a positive or a negative. People say all the time that life is rough. I used to say this often when I lost my way and forgot that it was my choice whether I lived a life I loved or a life of stress, worry, and frustration.

When you feel these negative reactions to life rise up in you, take a pause. Look at where these feelings are coming from and choose a different response to life. It may mean becoming present to who you have chosen to be. It may also mean choosing an empowering way of being in the moment. The choice is up to you. Reframe the context and you get to alter your experience of any moment. Be careful though, as this works both ways. You can talk yourself into believing that a really great moment wasn't really great just as easily as you can talk yourself into a not so great moment being a positive empowering experience.

It's all in your mind. Once you realize that you are the storyteller, life gets a lot more fun!!! Go out there and create a great story!

SECTION ONE

1

WHERE YOUR FOCUS GOES YOU GO

Life Lessons:

1. What you focus on grows. So... Create something amazing to focus on. Focus on things you want to grow and multiply.
2. Where your focus goes, you go. So... Set goals that focus you in the direction you want to go.
3. What you focus on, you'll create. So... Focus on and even dream about what you want to create.
4. What you look for, you'll find. So... Search for the things you want to find in life. Search for the good in people and the world around you.
5. Focus solely on the positive to grow the positive things in your life.
   a. Be grateful for what you're happy you have and you'll get more of those positive things in your life.
   b. Focus on things you don't like or want and you'll get more of those.
   c. So... Choose to focus on the positive.
6. Focusing on taking care of you is as important as any other goal.
7. So... Focus on showing yourself, love.

Action Steps:

1. Create a list of things that light you up, things you love. Here's an example of some things I love: sunsets, singing, dancing, hiking, travelling, and playing cards with friends and family.
2. Create a list of the monetary or physical goals you are working towards. Here are a few of mine to get you started: healthy living, great relationships, passive income sufficient to travel and making a difference in the world.
3. What will having those things provide for your life?
4. What is your vision of a perfect life?
5. What is your vision of a perfect world?
6. Describe your perfect relationship?
7. Describe your perfect day?
8. Go start creating them!

2

WHO WOULD YOU HAVE TO BE?

Life Lessons:

1. It all starts with a way of 'being'.
2. The best feeling is when you own your new way of being.
3. When you feel a new way of being from your heart; you have it.
4. 'Being' starts with the heart.
5. Think: Who would I have to 'be' to 'have' everything I want?
6. Your way of 'being' gives you the actions to 'do'.
7. Your 'doing' gives you the results you want in life or what you 'have'.
8. 'Be' the 'you', you've always wanted to 'be' and you'll begin to 'do' the things necessary to 'have' what you've always wanted.
9. Think - Be, Do, Have.
10. You Be You, The World Will Adjust!

Action Steps:

8. Invent a new way of being to live and take action from.
   a. The answer to the question "Who are you?" always starts with I am... not I'm becoming or I want to be. Just a simple declaration... I am... 'fill in the blank.' Speak it into existence. For Example: Since learning this technique, I have created several new ways of being
      i. Before my marriage I created - I am free, open, playful and passionate.
      ii. Recently, while working on getting back to my healthy self, I created - I am a beautiful, loving, healing, passionate woman.
   b. Answer the following questions in your journal:
      i. Who would I have to 'be' to love my life now?
      ii. What type of person would it take to create the results I am now focused on and truly want in my life?
      iii. How would it feel to have what you want?
      iv. How would you act if you had attained your goal?
      v. What actions would you naturally take?
      vi. What ways of being will you now create for yourself?
      vii. So... Who Are You?
9. Each morning take a moment to close your eyes and imagine yourself already having the results you want in life.
10. Throughout the day as you are faced with choices as to what actions to take in your life, ask yourself silently or out loud: What would a (insert your inspiring way of being here) do? For Example: What would a free, open, playful and passionate person do right now in this situation?
    a. It's ok to imagine what someone else would do until you start imagining yourself doing these things.
    b. Then think of/imagine yourself doing the same thing.
    c. Once you have it in mind, take the action you see needed coming from your new way of being

11. Choose an action item from your list that you are committed to take on consistently from your new way of being, towards your desired results for at least the next 21 days. (It takes 21 days to build a habit) Go for it!

12. The easiest way to take this on will be to take on foming one habit that comes from your new way of being a month. You can go faster if you like and take on a new one every 21 days or even sooner. However, it's nice to give yourself time to cement in place your new habits and ways of being.

13. Be sure to write down the habits you plan to cultivate, the actions that will have you take and the results you expect to create through forming this new habit. Again you can use your own journal or purchase the journal and/or workbook that go with this book. The Journal has inspirational quotes and thought-provoking questions to help you along your journey. The workbook has every question here with room to write out your answers.

www.ILoveMyselfSo.com will direct you to the Amazon Page with the I Love Myself So Quotes & Questions Journal as well as the workbook.

3

ENJOY EVERY MOMENT

Life Lessons:

1. Be present.
2. Enjoy every moment.
3. Experience your moments your way.
4. Swim with the current versus upstream. Go with the flow of life.
5. Hit the pause button and take your time. Soak in every second.

Action Steps:

1. Take time out in the evening to take note of a beautiful moment

you experienced throughout your day. As you begin to do this each night you may find that you begin noticing the moments as they happen versus having to reflect back on the day to remember them.

2. Being to plan out moments like the day I described above. These moments will allow you to practice being present and truly enjoying each second.

3. Practice makes perfect. So... keep practicing these until you start to notice when you aren't present. Being present is key to loving your life.

4. Write out a few examples of moments you can imagine creating for yourself to enjoy.

4

ACCEPT WHAT IS

Notes:

1. Follow your gut. It's usually right.
2. Sometimes it just your time to be reminded of a lesson.
3. Check insurance coverages/riders if you have expensive jewelry.
4. You may want to lock away your valuables when renting out your spare room to a person you don't fully know yet.
5. You may want to hire a property manager if you have rentals. They are a more impersonal way to approach rental ownership. The cost can save you stress, frustration and time. However, I love knowing my tenants. However I now always Do Background Checks and get a down payment before allowing a rental candidate to stay in any of my properties and especially my own home. In several cases, I trusted my gut and chose renters who may not have looked great on paper with credit checks, but were perfect in real life. In fact, some who traditional evaluations would say looked the worst, turned out to be the best! Do your homework and get training or one on one coaching if you plan to purchase and/or manage investment properties.

Life lessons:

1. Accept what is.
2. Expect Miracles.
3. Let go to let the miracles flow!
4. Stuff is far less important than happiness.
5. Things don't just happen, they happen just right.
6. Let karma do its work so you are free to enjoy your life.
7. Embrace the storms of life and learn to dance in the rain.
8. Letting go of any negative things currently taking up space in your mind will allow space for you to start appreciating the little things that make life beautiful.
9. Look for the empowering reasons, amazing lessons or opportunities provided when 'seemingly' bad things happened.

Action Steps:

1. You can now look back at things that have frustrated you in the past that you haven't let go of in a new light. Also, when you start to get frustrated in life, stop and think before you act: Use these steps for future as well as past frustrations you have in life.
   a. What actually happened?
   b. What good can getting frustrated accomplish?
   c. What negative consequences will my frustration have?
   d. What responsibility do I need to take in this situation?
      i. Did my actions in part or I full cause this?
      ii. Did I think of what the other person might have been going through in the situation? If so, how did I? If not, how can I in the future?
   e. What are the positive takeaways here?
      i. What can I do differently in the future?
      ii. What lessons can I learn here?
      iii. What good came out of it?
   f. How can I now reframe this incident in a positive light?

5

WORDS ARE KEYS TO UNLOCK YOUR DREAMS

Life Lessons:

1. Your words create your world.
2. Your words can be windows or barricades to your dreams.
3. Your words can give you more of what you want or more of what you are trying to avoid. You choose in the words you use.
   a. Use your words to praise and appreciate what you love and want in your life and you'll get more of it.
   b. Use your words to condemn and complain about what you dislike or detest in life and you'll get more of that.

Action Steps:

1. Write down everything you love in and about your life.
2. Write down everything you love about your body, mind and spirit.
3. Write down all the words you could use and every action you could take to show yourself, love.
4. Write down the word and actions you could use to show love to those in your life.
5. Start taking those actions and saying those things and watch the love in your life grow exponentially.
6. Speak with the intention to create what you want. Start calling your desires to you. You will begin to see them materialize.
7. Remember to be grateful for all that you receive and create.

6

BE RIGHT OR BE HAPPY

Life lessons:

1. You can either 'be right' or 'be happy.'
2. Accept the people in your life the way they are.
3. Learn to be quiet and listen for other people's greatness.
4. You can improve any relationship by altering only your actions.
5. Your most challenging person can bless you with your biggest lesson.
6. You are who you hang around. Some habits are 'hangingarounditary.'
7. 'Shoulding' on yourself accomplishes nothing but creating regrets.

Action steps:
Journal on the following topics:

1. Write down all of the times you feel mentally or physically exhausted, anxious, stressed and/or frustrated.
    a. Identification is the first step.
    b. Frustration indicates an area of life where you're doing something that doesn't work.
    c. Where are you frustrated in life?
2. Identify possible causes for your challenges and frustrations.
    a. What could you have been doing to cause these feelings?
    b. What things have you been doing that don't work for you?
    c. Create alternate actions you feel work in these situations.
    d. Be sure these actions from your new way of being.
    e. Write these moments down each time you notice them and the alternative actions you can take in the future.
3. Work to notice when you're in the midst of these situations and pause to substitute your alternate action.

4. Work to notice before you reach one of these situations and choose an alternate response for that situation as the moment arises.
5. Evaluate the results you get by implementing these new actions.
    a. If you like the results rinse and repeat.
    b. If the results are unfavorable choose other actions.
    c. Test your new actions in the next challenging situation.
    d. Keep going until you get the desired results.
6. Begin to make the difference and choose to love your life.
7. Refer to Dale Carnegie's book, "How to Win Friends & Influence People," for more information on this subject and more.

7

SHARE YOUR GIFTS

Life lessons:

1. The more you do anything the easier it gets.
2. In order that share your gifts in a way that makes a difference, you must come from a loving place.
    a. People don't care how much you know until they know how much you care.
    b. Seek first to understand before seeking to be understood.
    c. Refer again to Dale Carnegie's book, "How to Win Friends & Influence People," or Steven Covey's "The Seven Habits of Highly Effective People" for more information on this subject.
3. Buddha taught five things to consider before speaking. Is what you're saying:
    a. Factual and true
    b. Helpful or beneficial
    c. Spoken with kindness and good-will (that is, hoping for the best for all involved)
    d. Endearing (that is, spoken gently, in a way the other person can hear)

    e. Timely (occasionally something true, helpful, and kind will *not* be endearing, or easy for someone to hear, in which case we think carefully about *when* to say it)

Action steps:

1. List your gifts.
   a. What do you feel you were born to share with the world?
   b. What do you get compliments on?
   c. What do people thank you for?
2. In what ways do you already share your gifts?
3. List other ways you can share your gifts with the world.
4. How do your gifts make a difference for you and for others?
5. Practice pausing after someone stops speaking for a few reasons:
   a. They may not be finished.
   b. You then have time to consider your response.
      i. Be slow to criticize.
      ii. Start with a positive word.
      iii. Acknowledge what they've said first.
         1. It shows them respect.
         2. It allows them to feel heard.
         3. It also makes certain you understood.
         4. Your response can then be more easily accepted and heard.
   c. When in doubt think:
      i. How do I want this conversation to turn out?
      ii. How will my words affect this relationship?
      iii. How can I make a positive impact?

8

P E R F E C T L Y   I M P E R F E C T

Life Lessons:

1. Accept your perfect imperfection and that of others.
2. Let go of judgment, fear and worrying what others think and you'll let go of stress and enjoy life!
3. Give compliments freely and often. You never know how much it will mean to the person receiving them.
4. What other people think of you is none of your business unless it benefits you. Constructive criticism is a great tool when requested. However, check in with your intuition to be sure that their suggestions are a fit for the direction you are choosing for your life before acting upon anyone's opions or advice. Create your own opinions and run with them.
   a. Pay attention to common sense and decency. As long as your version of fun is only affecting you and others in a positive way, you're fine.
   b. When your fun affects someone else, then their opinion does matter. Be respectful, courteous and treat others as you feel they'd want to be treated.
5. "Treat others as *you* would want to be treated" is the Golden Rule. In the lesson above, I'm referring to the Platinum Rule. "Treat others as *they* want to be treated."
6. Pay attention and ask questions and get to know the people in your life. This will help you in so many areas.
7. Everything is better when you're doing something you love.
8. Surround yourself with great people and your life will continue to improve!
9. Life is a choice! You can choose to love it and live it powerfully!
10. Let your perfectly imperfect light shine and brighten the world, freeing other so do the same as well!

Action Steps:

1. Check out these sources for more information on the above lessons. Look into learning more about the people that you love and work with. Discover their Love Languages, Color Codes, Meyers Briggs or DISC types. These sources can assist you in relating to and using 'The Platinum Rule' to treat them the way they want to be treated.
   a. How to Win Friends and Influence People - Dale Carnegie
   b. Don't Sweat the Small Stuff - Richard Carlson
   c. The Four Agreements - Don Miguel Ruiz
   d. The 5 Languages of Love - Gary Chapman
   e. The Myers Briggs test - mbtionline.com
   f. The DISC test - discpersonalitytesting.com
   g. The Color Code- Taylor Hartman
      i. Taylor Hartman books
      ii. The Color Code Online Personality Test
   h. The Platinum Rule - Dr. Tony Alessandra-
      i. www.alessandra.com/abouttony/aboutpr.asp
      ii. www.youtube.com/tonyalessandra
      iii. youtu.be/rRB-504Wn3M
2. Write down several options to fill in the blank after this statement.
   a. I Love Myself So...
   b. So... What?
   c. Create something to fill in the '...' for yourself.
   d. What would you do right now if you truly loved you?
   e. Use this question or these answers to inspire you the next time you have a choice to make.

SECTION TWO

9

REINVENTING YOU

Life Lessons:

1. You can reinvent yourself at any point!
2. You're never stuck with anything you create.
3. Don't let anyone hold you back from being who you truly want to be.
4. You can always create something that inspires and empowers you!

Action Steps:

1. Who are you? Take some time to write down how you see yourself right now. By this, I mean all of the amazing qualities you already possess.
2. Who do you long to be? Take some time to write down all of the qualities you'd like to cultivate in yourself.
3. Who in your life has these qualities that you admire?
4. What results or things do they have that you long for?
5. What your life would look like if you were this person you long to be?
   a. Write down a description of a day in your perfect life.
   b. Describe yourself as the person you long to be in the present tense. Example: I am free, fun, engaging and charismatic.
   c. What would you be doing?
   d. List some results that are important to you?

10

SEIZE OPPORTUNITIES

Life Lessons:

1. Expect miracles.
2. Seize Opportunities.
3. Look for ways to create miracles.
4. Look for ways to connect with people.
5. Seek first to understand, then to be understood.
6. Look for ways to bring joy to others. In doing so you'll naturally create joy in your own life.
7. Cherish time with loved ones because you never know how long you'll have them in your life.

Action Steps: Answer these questions in your journal:

1. Where in your life do you see opportunities to connect with people?
2. Where are you taking advantage of those opportunities?
3. What more can you do about that? Where can you connect?
4. Where might you be missing out on opportunities and experiences to connect in your life?
5. How would seizing opportunities impact your life for the better?
6. Refer to Steven Covey's "7 Habits of Highly Effective People" for more information on seeking first to understand, then to be understood.
7. Refer to "The Secret" by Rhonda Byrne to learn about expecting, attracting and creating miracles.

11

OUT OF THE COMFORT ZONE
A Year of Exploration

Life Lessons:

1. Listen to your gut.
2. Look for opportunities to enjoy new experiences.
3. Get out of your comfort zone.
4. Plan for your dreams.
5. Spend less than you earn.
6. Save for expenses or create an escape route for any debt incurred.
7. Do what's necessary to maintain or improve your credit score.

Action Steps:
Work on these questions in your journal:

1. What places or things have you always wanted to visit or experience?
2. What memories have you always wanted to make?
3. Where are you holding yourself back in life?
4. What would you do if you had an unlimited supply of money?
5. What would you do if you had time freedom?
6. What would it take for you to make those things happen for you given your current circumstances?
7. What negative mindset or beliefs would you need to let go of to allow your dreams to become reality?
8. What empowering belief will you create now to shift your focus to believing in yourself and your ability to create what you want in life?
9. What actions will you take to keep that belief in the forefront of your thoughts?
    a. Will you read it aloud each day?
    b. Will you write it out each day?
    c. Will you put it on a mirror so you see it each morning?

      d.   Will you write it on a notecard to keep with you all day?

      e.   Will you do all of the above?

10. What structures will you need in place to assist you in creating this new reality for yourself?

      a.   Will you tell a few friends or family members so they can hold you accountable?

      b.   Will you write out all the action steps and milestones?

      c.   Will you find a partner to go the distance with you?

12

ALWAYS BE CREATING
Two Tickets to Paris

Life Lessons:

1. Always Be Creating-
      a.   Continuously create so you have a future calling to you.
      b.   Your future reminds you of who you are committed to 'be.'
      c.   Your way of 'being' gives you the actions to take.
      d.   The actions you take, what you 'do' constitutes your 'doing.'
      e.   The actions you choose bring you the results you'll 'have.'
      f.   Keep this cycle going and you will remember who you are.

2. Be Flexible-
      a.   When life throws you a curve, choose your response.
      b.   Choosing your response gives you a say in the matter of life.
      c.   Use that space between the stimulus and your response wisely and choose a response to improves your life situation.
      d.   Those moments are your opportunities to shape your

future.

    e. Your response determines your level of happiness.

    f. Your response determines your direction.

    g. Your response determines your results.

3. Bounce Back-
   a. Be Open to change.
   b. Be thorough in assessing situations.
   c. Be willing to create new goals and dreams.
   d. Be strong enough to take action and move forward.

4. Know your 'why'-
   a. Your 'why' is the reason or purpose behind your actions.
   b. It will give meaning and direction to your steps each day.
   c. Your 'why' can come from or inspire your way of being.
   d. It will allow you to do all the things above when faced with the twists and turns of life.
   e. Your 'why' can change as life goes on. You may have several 'whys' that your life revolves around.

Action Steps:

1. Write down your new way of being again and come from there for these exercises.

2. What's Your 'Why'? Begin writing down ideas in your journal. Here are a few questions and an example to get you started.
   a. What keeps you going when you don't want to go?
   b. What currently gives you purpose?
   c. What inspires you in life?
   d. What calls to you?
   e. What do you want most?
   f. My 'why' is making a difference and loving my life.
      i. It gets me out of bed.
      ii. It calls to me and inspires me.
      iii. It gives me purpose and direction.
      iv. It enhances and gives my life meaning.

3. What goal or dream can you see with your new way of being and your 'why' in mind?

4. Choose a specific day in the future by which you are committed to achieving this goal. Imagine you've attained that goal. What

year is it? Write down what you have on that day as if you already have it.

    a. Describe the day in the first person and present tense so that anyone reading the statement could easily see that you've achieved your desired results.

    b. What do you have now as a result of coming from the new way of being you created in the past chapter?

    c. You may be describing:

        i. A day in the place you want to visit.

        ii. A home you plan to purchase.

        iii. A day with the person you love.

        iv. A night you win an award.

        v. Or you may be going for an entirely different dream.

    d. Now that you have your results, from there, look back at the path you created over that year to lead you to this moment.

    e. What steps do you now see necessary to reach your goals?

    f. What milestones will you have reached at six months?

    g. What results can you create in the next month?

    h. What can you create this week?

5. Where else can you use this process in your life?

    a. Start making note of other goals and dreams.

    b. Write them down as you think of them daily.

    c. You'll use these to expand your list in the goals chapter.

13

CHOOSE YOUR ATTITUDE

Life Lessons:

1. People don't make you happy. You make you happy.
2. Stuff doesn't make you happy. You make you happy.
3. When grey clouds of turmoil enter your life, take a new approach. You can always find a silver lining if you search for it.
4. Remember, you get what you're looking for. Look for the good in every situation and every person you meet.
5. You attract what you focus on. Focusing on the positives will help you draw amazing things into your life. So...start using positive focus to your advantage.

Warning: Search for good, but still pay attention to possible red flags. This means to be a good finder. Follow your gut, but keep your eyes open to possibly dangerous situations. Do your due diligence.

Divorce Lessons:

1. I can handle anything!
2. I can be a minimalist.
3. I can live almost anywhere.
4. I can reinvent myself at any moment.
5. I can choose my response in any situation.
6. I can take what I'm given and create an amazing life from nothing!
7. I can be happy regardless of the circumstances in my life.
8. Accepting what is, versus getting stuck in what was, or attached to how I think it should be, is everything in life!
9. I can create powerful goals and dreams that give me purpose and call me forward into living a life I love and living it powerfully NO MATTER WHAT!
10. I can take the next step in the face of not knowing the end result.

By knowing who I am and keeping my focus on my goal I can move forward. All there is to do is choose who I'm going to be in the moment and take action from that manner of being. I can be courageous, loving, accepting, adventurous or any other way of being that empowers me.

Action Steps:

1. Make a list of the great things in your life. Continue to add to it as often as possible.
2. Make lists of all the great things about the people in your life. Add to your list as often as you think of things.
3. Make a list of the great things about you and add to it as often as possible.
4. Make a list of opportunities where you see you might simplify your life to create more space for the things that matter.
5. Add to these lists as often as possible, ideally every day in your journal to continue to focus on the positive in your life to keep your attitude focused in the right direction.

14
GET YOUR GOALS TO WORK ON YOU

Life Lessons:

1. Share your goals; get the universe working for you.
2. Do your due diligence when planning for your goals.
3. Figure out how you work best and play to your strengths.
4. Go with your gut. Do what feels right to you.
5. Find and use strategies that work for you.
6. Choose your battles.
7. Get it in writing.

Action Steps:

1. Make a list of all the goals you've achieved in your life.
2. Make a list of the goals you are working on.
3. Make a list of your dreams.
4. Give them each a deadline or date by which you'll complete them.
5. Now look back and follow the steps from chapter seven for each to create milestones with a timeline for each goal you've listed.
6. Now that they're in your mind, let them go to work on you! Your subconscious can now assist you in bringing about what you are thinking about!
7. Get into action! It has been said by some that the Lord helps those who help themselves. You must act on as well as think about your goals.

15
CELEBRATE YOUR WINS

Life Lessons:

1. Taking time to celebrate your wins has several benefits.
   a. It reminds you to feel good about your achievements.
   b. It gives you a reward to look forward to attaining goals.
   c. It can also assist in planning your next goal as in my case.
2. Turn your stumbling blocks into stepping stones that you can stand on to reach your goals.
3. Delayed gratification feels amazing.

Action Steps:

1. Write down possible rewards or celebrations for reaching goals in your life:
   a. List a few little ones that don't require much to produce.

     i.   A massage

    ii.   A night out with friends to celebrate

   iii.   A simple walk in the park to enjoy the sunset

   iv.   Anything you've wanted to do or to acquire but haven't spent the money or time to acquire or enjoy.

b. Create a few that would be a worthy celebration for big goals.

     i.   A vacation like mine

    ii.   An expensive accessory like a watch or set of jewelry, a suit or dress or perhaps a whole new wardrobe

   iii.   Any large purchases you've put off till now

16

STEPPING STONES TO EUROPE

Life Lessons:

1. If you stumble on your stepping stones you can use those stumbling blocks to build a staircase to reach your next goal.
2. Turn your challenges into growth opportunities.
3. Look for life to help you along and it will.
4. Listen to your heart.
5. Enjoy the Journey.
6. Live your dreams.
7. Go with the flow.
8. Fail forward.

Action Steps:

1. Where in your life are you facing challenges?
2. How can you reframe these challenges as opportunities?
3. Describe a time you felt like everything went your way.
   a. How did it feel?
   b. What mindset did you have leading up to it?
   c. Were you thinking everything would work out?
4. Look back and make a list of the times that life has given you a helping hand.
5. Keep reframing challenges and growing to reach your goals. Soon you'll begin to naturally think from this winning attitude.
6. Look back and list challenges you now see to learn and grow from.
7. What challenges can you step up on to reach your next goal?
   a. Look at your list of goals from Chapter 14.
   b. List challenges you see that you may face.
   c. Now list ways you can overcome these!
8. Continue to grow and work on you. Growth is a never-ending

process. You can always learn. Kaisen = Constant and never-ending improvement. Remember, you are either growing or you are dying.

9. Start loving your life now! Take action and go through the lessons and actions steps in the book. I've summarized here in this last chapter. This summary will make it easy to refer back for a quick lesson or so you can continue to update your answers as your life changes. If you'd like even more support in taking action you can purchase the journal or workbook at www.ILoveMyselfSo.com

10. **Quick Summary**

   a. Refer back to this book whenever you have a challenge. Read the chapter that applies to that challenge and it will remind you what to do in the moment.

   b. Listen to your heart and focus on what you truly desire and allow it to begin to come to you naturally.

   c. Remember, that what drives you in any given moment may change. In order to move forward, it works best to go with the flow and accept that change is a part of life.

   d. Embrace your perfect imperfection and accept the assistance when need. Be it from family, a friend or a coach of some sort.

   e. Share what you've learned with the world. In sharing what you have learned you understand at a deeper level. In sharing you get to grow and develop yourself! It's the gift that gives back!

   f. **What could you do right now out of truly loving yourself?**

Go Do It!!!

Go Create A Life

You Love!!!!

ONLY YOU CAN
CREATE A LIFE YOU LOVE &
LIFE IT POWERFULLY
NO MATTER WHAT!

~ CORY JENKINS

ACKNOWLEDGMENTS

A huge thank you goes out to all the teachers I've learned from throughout my life. My family and friends, Landmark Education, T Harv Eker, Robert Allen, Les Brown, Impact Training, Trinity School of Nutrition, NSA the Makers of Juice Plus, Jim Rohn, Jack Canfield, Marianne Williamson, Napoleon Hill, Tony Robbins, Robert Kiyosaki, Og Mandino, Omar Periu, Bob Proctor, Robert Allen, Keith Cunningham, Greg Habstritt, Dave Sullivan, Les Brown, Tom Hopkins, Zig Ziglar, and so many more!

References

Education:

1. www.LandmarkEducation.com
2. www.impactslc.com

Books:

1. Success Principles - Jack Canfield
2. The 5 Languages of Love - Gary Chapman
3. The Color Code books- Taylor Hartman
4. How to Win Friends and Influence People - Dale Carnegie
5. Don't Sweat the Small Stuff - Richard Carlson
6. The Four Agreements - Don Miguel Ruiz
7. 7 Habits of Highly Effective People - Steven Covey

Videos & Assessments:

1. The Secret - Rhonda Byrne
2. The Color Code- online test- http://www.colorcode.com/choose_personality_test/
3. The Myers Briggs test - mbtionline.com
4. The DISC test - discpersonalitytesting.com
5. The Platinum Rule - Dr. Tony Alessandra-
   a. www.alessandra.com/abouttony/aboutpr.asp
   b. www.youtube.com/tonyalessandra
   c. youtu.be/rRB-504Wn3M

EPILOGUE

I have currently settled in Dunedin, Florida after traveling the U.S. and beyond visiting friends and searching for my next rental property location and home. If I travel through your town you may find me out enjoying one of my favorite hobbies. Since I love meeting new people, I will be out dancing swing, salsa, country or any other partner dance; maybe even tango. You may also catch me singing karaoke or even jumping in with a local band. During the day I may be hiking, biking or running to enjoy the great outdoors.

I'm setting up speaking engagements to share about creating a life you love. I have several other books in the pipeline that you can look forward to. To learn more about working with me you can either email me at Cory@ILoveMyselfSo.com or visit my Facebook page: www.Facebook.com/LoveYouToLifeCoach.

Below is the view from my friend's house in England which was one of my 'offices' while working on this book. I'll be headed back there to house sit and work on my next book "Love You to Life" while I live out its principles.

A GIFT FOR YOU

As a thank you and reward for taking time to work on you through my book, I would like to give you a discount on the Love You to Life course. This will take your experience with this book into your life in a more powerful way and expand your love for your life exponentially.

Simply Email me at **Cory@ILoveMyselfSo.com**. Use the subject line-Love You to Life Course Discount to receive information on your discount to the Love you to Life course by email.

ABOUT THE AUTHOR

Cory's travel bug has taken her to over 30 countries and soon to be every state. Her bucket list keeps growing and shrinking as she reaches her goals and sets new ones.

She owns rental properties and has been selling Juice Plus for over 20 years. She grew up in St. Louis, Missouri, lived all over the San Francisco Bay area and settled in Utah for over ten years to buy real estate between Ogden and Salt Lake City. While traveling all over the United States and abroad in search of her next investment property and working for Elite Online Publishing remotely she completed her certification as a life coach and created the Love You to Life Course. She eventually moved to Dunedin, Florida to expand her real estate portfolio and enjoyment of life. Stay tuned for the next chapter.

She is finally pursuing her dream of writing books and speaking to make a difference in people's lives. Look for new books and journals on her Amazon author page: www.Amazon.com/Author/CoryJenkins or on www.ILoveMyselfSo.com

For more information about working with Cory or setting up a speaking engagement you can contact her through her website or via email at Cory@ILoveMyselfSo.com. You can also connect with her through her Facebook page at: www.Facebook.com/LoveYouToLifeCoach. This will also connect you to the Love You to Life Facebook community so you get updates for any events as well as your regualar dose of inspiration.

Made in the USA
Columbia, SC
05 March 2020